Thoughts on Translation

the translation industry and becoming a translator

Corinne McKay

Thoughts on Translation: the translation industry and becoming a translator
by Corinne McKay

ISBN 978-0-578-10735-6

Disclaimer: This book is published by Two Rat Press and TranslateWrite, Inc., who acknowledge all trademarks. All information contained in this book is believed to be correct at the time of printing. However, readers are advised to seek professional advice where necessary, as the information in this book is based on the author's experiences. The author of this book is not professionally engaged in providing legal, financial or career planning advice. Please send comments or corrections to corinne@translatewrite.com.

Cover design: Sue Campbell
Layout and copyediting: Daniel J. Urist
Author photograph: Cameron Weise

Contents

Introduction   **7**

Acknowledgments and thanks   **9**

1 Getting started as a translator   11
1.1 How to get started as a translator   11
1.2 How to succeed as a freelance translator   13
1.3 Developing translation specializations   14
1.4 Marketing your services to translation agencies . .   16
1.5 Avoiding beginner's mistakes   18
1.6 The chicken or the egg?   20
1.7 Finding your first translation clients   22
1.8 Freelance translation FAQ   25
1.9 Some thoughts on test translations   27
1.10 My favorite mistake   29
1.11 The ten essentials of freelance translation   31

2 Growing your freelance business   33
2.1 The importance of aiming low   33
2.2 Book review: The Entrepreneurial Linguist   35
2.3 Review your professional association memberships   37
2.4 My favorite non-translation business books   38
2.5 Tips for a successful translation conference presentation   40
2.6 Some thoughts on setting goals   42
2.7 When to seek professional help   43
2.8 Break on through   45

3 Translation technique and translation quality   49
3.1 Which English?   49

3.2 Keeping up your source language skills 50
3.3 Translators and proofreading 51
3.4 Some thoughts on gender-neutral language 54
3.5 I feel like I've read this somewhere before 56
3.6 A little bit of this, a little bit of that 57
3.7 Some thoughts on translation specializations . . . 58

4 The freelance mindset   **61**
4.1 Shoshin 61
4.2 Are bad habits a form of self-protection? 63
4.3 Getting things done 64
4.4 The art of saying no 66
4.5 Twin Translations: A passion for languages 68
4.6 Finding the time 71
4.7 The second half 72
4.8 What types of incentives work best for you 73

5 Client relations   **77**
5.1 What to send clients and colleagues for the holidays 77
5.2 Easy versus cheap 79
5.3 Passing as "one of them": the client Turing test . . 81
5.4 Getting the names straight 83
5.5 Dear Client... 85
5.6 Using objective data to set your rates 87
5.7 Dispute resolution in the translation industry . . . 90
5.8 Vetting prospective clients and job offers 92
5.9 When a client is dissatisfied 94

6 Translation technology and home office setup   **97**
6.1 Options for home office phone service 97
6.2 Why you need good web hosting 99
6.3 Staying comfortable in the home office 100
6.4 Why netbooks are better than smartphones 102
6.5 Home or away? 104
6.6 Why I use free and open source software 105
6.7 Translation memory discounts: yes, no, maybe? . 107

7 Marketing and networking   **109**

7.1 LinkedIn strategies 109
7.2 Some thoughts on professional photographs . . . 110
7.3 Tips for promoting your freelance services 112
7.4 Translation-targeted resumés 113
7.5 Moving on up 115

8 Money matters 117
8.1 How much do freelancers earn? Is it enough? . . . 117
8.2 Putting 40 cents a word in context 119
8.3 Some thoughts on hourly and salaried pay 122
8.4 What about TM discounts? 123
8.5 Some thoughts on volume discounts 125
8.6 Supplier or demander? 126
8.7 Some thoughts on translation rates 128
8.8 Paid by the word or paid by the hour 129
8.9 Payments without borders 130
8.10 Tracking your freelance income 131
8.11 Some thoughts on financial management 133
8.12 ATA conference topic: low payers 135

9 Webinar questions 137
9.1 Small-diffusion languages 137
9.2 How many words per day? 138
9.3 Preparing for the ATA certification exams 140
9.4 Should I incorporate? 143
9.5 Does age matter? 145

Index 147

Introduction

In February, 2008, I launched the blog Thoughts on Translation www.thoughtsontranslation.com as a way to blend my interests in translation, writing and connecting with other translators. Over five years and several hundred posts later, it's proven to be a lively discussion forum for freelance translators around the world. During that time, the translation blogosphere has grown exponentially, and any given work day features translators blogging about technology, their specializations, their clients and nearly any hot news in the industry. Thoughts on Translation currently draws approximately 500 visitors per day, and I have really enjoyed writing it as both a creative outlet and as a way to connect with other translators, project managers and word people in general.

This book represents a compilation of most (but not all) of the 406 blog posts that I wrote between February, 2008 and January, 2012. All of these posts are still active on my blog, so if you'd like to contribute your own thoughts, just click over to www.thoughtsontranslation.com and add a comment!

Acknowledgments and thanks

My blog and thus this book would never have come into existence without the advice and encouragement of my friend and blogging guru Beth Hayden of Blogging With Beth. Thoughts on Translation was just a vague idea in my head when I took Beth's "Introduction to Blogging" course in early 2008, and she has continued to be an outstanding source of advice and inspiration since I started my blog.

A blog exists as part of the blogosphere, and I'm very grateful for the worldwide community of translation bloggers and authors of which I'm a part. Big thanks to Lisa Carter (Intralingo), Sarah Dillon (There's Something About Translation), Chris Durban (The Prosperous Translator), Sara Freitas (Les Recettes du Traducteur), Judy and Dagmar Jenner (Translation Times), Kevin Lossner (Translation Tribulations), Tony Rosado (The Professional Interpreter), Riccardo Schiaffino (About Translation), Jill Sommer (Musings from an Overworked Translator), Michael Wahlster (Translate This!) and Tess Whitty (The Business of Translation) for their comments, suggestions, fabulous posts, links and retweets and to my invaluable colleague Eve Lindemuth Bodeux for almost a decade of professional collaboration and friendship. My husband, my daughter and my parents are my anchor in the craziness of life, and for that, no thanks will ever be enough.

1 Getting started as a translator

1.1 How to get started as a translator

For beginning and experienced translators alike, there is often no way around the need to cold-contact potential clients. Beginners need to find those crucial first few clients, and those of us who are established in the industry may want to look for better-paying work, work with direct clients or work in a new specialization. As in any profession, a warm or hot contact is always the most attractive; a personal referral from a colleague or current client has a much higher success rate than an e-mail, phone call or letter out of the blue. However, there's no denying that cold contacting works when you want to launch or grow your translation business. Here are a few cold contacting techniques and some tips on how to apply them.

- Phone calls are of limited use as a first point of contact with a potential translation client. I think that a phone call is appropriate only in response to a job posting that lists a phone number, or if a potential client's other contact information (e-mail, mailing address etc.) is not available and you're simply making the call to get that information. If you make a phone call to a potential client, be like e-mail: introduce yourself, get to the point ("what would be the best way to send you my resumé?"), and then let the client go.

- Mass e-mail campaigns are another cold contacting technique that I would discourage. Although it's tempting to write a "dear agency" e-mail, attach your resumé and blast it off to a few hundred translation companies, this technique may a) be perceived as spam and simply deleted and b) appeal to the type of clients you don't really want to work for: low payers or clients who do not focus on quality.

- Personalized e-mail forms the backbone of most translators' initial marketing campaigns. Most translation companies have application instructions right on their website (look for a link to "contact," "freelancers" or "employment"), whereby you use either the agency's online form or send your application materials to an e-mail address that the agency provides. If you are sending a cover letter by e-mail, keep it very brief. Something along the lines of "To the attention of X translation company: I am a freelance X to X translator, and I am interested in offering my services to your agency. My specializations include X, X and X, and I have X years of experience working with X types of clients. In addition, I (am certified by X translators association, have a PhD in biology, am a CPA, worked in international trade for 10 years, etc.). My resumé is attached for your consideration and I look forward to speaking with you about how we might work together in the future."

- Postal mail is a technique that I think can work well with direct clients. When you're applying to a translation company, you don't have to convince the company that they need your services, but with a direct client you may. So, you may want to give the client more information than is appropriate to send in a cold e-mail; for example samples of your work, a brochure about your services, etc. Online printing services have also made it much easier to create professional-looking marketing postcards, and these are fast and inexpensive to create and send out to potential clients.

One element of cold contacting that translators often overlook is requesting a personal interview with local clients, or with clients who are in a city that you will be visiting. Especially if you are just starting your business but present yourself well in person, I think it can work very well to e-mail a potential client and ask if you can "stop in for a few minutes to learn more about their business and how you might fit in." Take a small gift and treat the meeting as an informational interview, where you are not so much trying to sell yourself as trying to find out what the client's needs are.

1.2 How to succeed as a freelance translator

I get a lot of e-mails from people who want to become translators. A typical contact is from someone who is bilingual and either doesn't enjoy his/her current job or because of necessity (i.e. a spouse whose job is repeatedly transferred) wants to find a profitable work-from-home job. Based on my own experience, the experience of other translators I work with and the students I've taught in my course for beginning translators, here are a few basic tips on how to become a translator and maybe more importantly, how to figure out if you really want to become a translator:

- Realistically evaluate your language skills and experience. Translators must have near-native command of their source ("from") language(s) and excellent writing skills in their target ("into") language(s). Unless you truly consider yourself a native speaker of two languages, don't try to translate in both "directions" and stick with translating from your non-native language into your native language.

- Realistically assess your ability to run a home-based business. The translation industry in the U.S. is heavily geared toward independent contractors, and the few in-house positions that exist are often intended for experienced translators only. Be honest with yourself about whether, in addition to being a good translator, you can be an effective marketer, customer service rep, accountant, office manager, etc.

- Plan for your startup phase. I've met translators who had a full-time freelance business up and running in just months, but these people mostly had strong contacts in the industry or worked in very in-demand specializations or language pairs. For the rest of us, a startup phase of six months to a year is more realistic. Plan ahead for how you'll support yourself (financially and mentally!) during this phase of intense marketing.

- Be ready for a marketing marathon. As I tell every student in my online course, I contacted over 400 potential clients during my first year as a freelance translator, and it still took 18 months until I was replacing the income from my previous full-time job. Be ready to pound the electronic pavement until you develop a stable of regular clients.

- Check out the competition. The best and easiest way to find out what other translators in your language pair charge, who their clients are and what specializations they work in is to hit the web. Do a search for translators in your language pair and see what they're up to (and what you can do better!).

- Enjoy it! By any measure, the translation industry is booming, and the demand for qualified translators far outstrips the supply in most language combinations. There are various compensation surveys for the translation industry, but personally I feel that with assertive marketing and high-quality service, income of at least US$75,000 a year is realistic. Given the job's flexibility, intellectual stimulation and growth potential, it's an outstanding field for bilingual people.

1.3 Developing translation specializations

Here's a great question that I received from reader Dorota Krysinska. She asks: *"... could you explain in your blog how it happened that you started specializing in legal, corporate communications and public health/international development translations? Did you have any background in these fields? I have been wondering how someone like me, who has done her degree in linguistic studies can begin to specialize as a translator in areas that she hasn't studied at all. Also, how do I go about sending out my resumé to translation agencies and not having any particular field of translation specified there?"*

The issue of specializations seems to come up a lot in our industry, so I'll offer my answer here. When I started translating, I was in pretty much the same boat as Dorota; I had a Master's in French Literature and had used French in my job (teaching high school) for eight years so I was reasonably confident about my language skills. In addition, I've always loved to write and I had done sideline work writing for magazines and had even worked in the editorial department of a book review publication in the summer. However, I didn't have an obvious area of specialization. I think that this can be a plus and a minus: in one sense, I really envied (and still sometimes do!) people who became translators after having worked in banking, law, pharmaceuticals, engineering, etc. because they are immediately able to jump in to a very specialized field. On the other hand, I think that someone who starts out as a generalist has a lot more opportunities to experiment with various specializations than someone who is fairly locked in to a certain field.

One of the best pieces of advice I've heard about specializations came from Jill Sommer (`www.translationmusings.com`), who said "Pick an area that you enjoy researching." In that vein, I've always had a secret (or now not so secret!) desire to go to law school. For whatever reason, I just love reading legal documents and deciphering the jargon in them. "Party of the first part..." "notwithstanding..." "pursuant to..." "aforementioned..." I don't know, I just enjoy it. Similarly, I enjoy reading the business news so corporate communications was a good fit for me, and I read a lot about health topics as well, hence my translation focus on public health. On the contrary, hard science has just never been my thing. I like science as an idea, I like listening to science stories on NPR, I enjoy translating "lighter" science documents about health and wellness, but give me a chemical patent and my eyes glaze over almost immediately.

So, I think the number one rule if you start out as a generalist is to pick documents that you enjoy reading and researching. Also, I think it can be helpful to identify some of your non-specializations as well. When I work with direct clients who have a wide range of documents, I sometimes tell them what I don't do (patents, anything having to do with engineering or technical specifications, heavy financial documents) so that they know if I am a good fit for them.

When it comes to contacting translation companies, I think it's best to be completely honest and differentiate between specializations in which you have experience and specializations in which you are interested. I don't think there's anything wrong with telling the client that although you've never translated in the area of X, you are very interested in X topic in your own language and you know a lot about the terminology (this once landed me a job translating the script for a promotional video about rock climbing ropes). Also, I don't think there's anything wrong with saying "I'm just starting my business so I'm open to working in a variety of specializations; some of my areas of interest are..."

1.4 Marketing your services to translation agencies

Whether to work with direct clients, translation agencies or both is a personal and business decision. I work with both types of clients and I feel that this mix keeps my work volume and income up while giving me a wide range of projects to choose from. Paula Dieli's blog (editorial note: this blog is no longer active) has an insightful interview with Peter Berends, the primary translator recruiter at LUZ, Inc. (a medical translation company). It's well worth a read if you're looking for agency clients. Here are some additional tips!

- Target your marketing. As Peter comments in the interview, there's no bigger turnoff than a generic, carbon-copied e-mail asking for work. The more personalized your e-mail is, the better. For example, something like "Your agency's focus on the translation of annual reports caught my eye; during the 2010 annual report season I translated all or part of five companies' annual reports and I would love to help you with similar types of projects" is much more attention-grabbing than "Dear Sir or Madam, I would like to offer you my services."

- Don't lump all agencies together. Yes, in general agencies pay less than direct clients and also add a middle layer between the translator and the client (which can be a plus or a minus depending on the project and the client). However, top-quality agencies pay respectably and can save you some of the administrative overhead that comes with working for direct clients. Just as in every other business sector, there are agencies that operate on the Wal-Mart model and agencies that operate on the Mercedes-Benz model.

- Charge real money and earn it. I think that a lot of translators eschew the agency market because they think it's all eight cents a word and 5,000 words for tomorrow. Insider tip: it's not. I think that quality-conscious agencies know that quality-conscious translators save them money because their work needs less editing and they help keep the agency's own clients coming back. Give some metrics of your quality: you proofread a hard copy of every translation (no missing text, no untranslated text); you compile a list of queries and send them all at once, allowing time to get the queries resolved before the deadline (no endless stream of e-mails to the already-busy project manager, no file submitted right at the deadline with queries still outstanding); you always meet or beat your deadlines (no panicked project manager having to make excuses to the end client).

- Focus on high-margin projects. For example if you actively seek out projects on which you can produce 500 finished words per hour and you charge 15 cents per word, you're earning $75 per hour. I think that it's also fine to let your agency clients know that you are most interested in medium to large projects, for example $500 or more. High-margin projects can also come in unexpected places, such as translating official documents. Each invoice might be small, but on most official document translations I make at least 50 cents per word.

- Use the objective data that is available to you. Don't market to agencies as if you're throwing spaghetti against a wall; pick some agencies that mesh with your business goals and market just to them. For example, search the Payment Practices (www.paymentpractices.net) database to find agencies that are rated highly by other translators.

- In general, target small and medium agencies. Not every big agency is a sweatshop, but I think that in general, large agencies are geared toward the high volume, low margin market. In addition, you're more likely to find small and medium agencies that work primarily or exclusively in your specializations.

1.5 Avoiding beginner's mistakes

Today is the first day of the winter session of the online course I teach for beginning translators. It's an occasion that always prompts me to remember the first day I thought of myself as a translator, and what I did correctly and incorrectly during that stressful and exciting first year as a freelancer. I've been mulling over some of the best and worst decisions I made when I first started freelancing. Here I'm mainly including advice for people who are in their first year of freelancing, but some of these tips apply to experienced translators as well.

DO keep a record of all of your contacts. During the first year you'll be doing a lot of marketing; at times during my first year, I was doing about 80% marketing and 20% translation. Trust me; a lot of this effort is wasted if you don't have a good system for tracking who you've contacted, what the response was (if any) and how you followed up if there was a response. This could take the form of a computerized contact management system, a spreadsheet, or even a Rolodex-type file, but make sure you save this information.

DO NOT take on work that you know is wrong for you just because you need work. This is a mistake that I made several times during my beginner days. For example, at one point I let a client convince me to translate into French and then have my work proofed by a native speaker. This resulted in a lower hourly rate for me since I write very slowly in French, and also in a lower-quality end product than what the client would have received from a native French speaker. At the time I remember thinking "... well, if the client thinks it's OK... " whereas now this is one of my non-negotiables no matter what the client says; I translate into English only.

DO ask prospective clients in your local area for an informational interview. To give my beginner self some credit, this is one thing that I think I did well. I e-mailed a variety of prospective clients in the Boulder/Denver, Colorado area and asked if I could come in to learn some more about their business and how I might, at some point, fit in. I think that this took the pressure off the prospective client because I wasn't aggressively pumping them for work, and I also correctly theorized that I presented myself better in person than on paper. Of the five or so prospective clients I visited, I ended up getting work from three of them soon after.

DO NOT contact agency owners directly. Of the beginner mistakes I made, this one was probably the worst; I used the local translator's association directory to find local agencies, then I phoned up the owners. Now I realize that although association directories and client websites are a great resource, wasting someone's time is a very poor first impression. Always use the general contact information provided on a prospective client's website, and avoid cold phone calls in nearly every situation.

DO ask for very specific instructions on your first few projects. Unless you've misrepresented your experience, the majority of your clients will realize that you're a beginner and won't mind doing a little hand-holding. So ask them: what do they mean by "reproduce the formatting exactly"? Should you do something special with handwritten text? What if something is illegible? What if there are abbreviations that you don't understand?

DO NOT set your rates suspiciously low. I think that especially in a down economy, many beginning freelancers are tempted to set their rates markedly below the going rate for their languages. I still cringe at some of the rates I accepted when I was first starting out. In one sense, I think that offering attractive terms can help get your business off the ground; in another sense, I think that lowball rates attract bottom-feeding clients who are looking for high-quality work for minimum wage. Personally, I think it's a better idea to sweeten your offer in other ways; maybe offering night or weekend work without a rush charge, or being available on holidays when other translators aren't working.

DO set reasonable expectations for the growth and success of your business. Of all the advice I give beginners, I would tag this as the most important. I've been contacted many times by beginning translators who say that they're "so discouraged" because they've sent out 25 applications in the last month and they still have no work. In my own case, I contacted over 400 prospective clients during my first year in business and it still took about 18 months until I was replacing the income from my previous full-time job. I think that for most people, it takes at least a year to get your business to the point where you are working more than you are looking for work; once you break through this point, you will hopefully have a freelance business that becomes like a regular job, except that you have a great deal of control over your schedule and income.

1.6 The chicken or the egg?

I've noticed that for many beginning translators, getting those first few clients is a chicken and egg issue; most agencies, which form the bulk of most beginners' client bases, aren't eager to work with translators who are very inexperienced. But if clients won't work with you, how do you ever get enough experience to make your business viable?

- Volunteer: Places such as legal aid agencies, refugee assistance centers, public health clinics and schools are often in need of volunteer linguists. Or, think strategically: that cute little B&B you stayed in on your trip to France last summer might love to have an English website done for free in exchange for a glowing testimonial about your work and a free weekend's stay. Just make sure to treat volunteer assignments with the same care you would paying ones.

- Start small: Many individuals need a translator for a project that is too small to be worth an agency's time, for example a birth certificate, driver's license, school transcript, etc. These projects tend to be very straightforward and can be very profitable because the actual amount of text is small. I get a lot of inquiries from my website for work like this, and you could also promote your services through your local consulates, cultural associations, bilingual schools, immigration attorneys, etc.

- Team up: Working with an experienced translator in your own language combination can work in a few ways. First, you could offer to pay an experienced translator's hourly rate to give you small practice translations and then edit them until your work is client-worthy. Not everyone is going to be interested in doing this, but some experienced translators enjoy this type of work. Second, if your translation skills are strong but you don't have much experience, you might find an experienced translator who needs a backup translator to work on small projects, overflow work, etc. Obviously this kind of arrangement has to be carefully crafted between two people with similar work styles and personalities, but it's a good reason to network in your local translators association.

- Start big: This requires careful planning, but I think that in some cases, people with high-level skills in specialized subject areas can do better by bypassing the standard paths completely and going straight for high-paying work with direct clients. For example, I've had two bilingual attorneys as students in my online translation class. Both of them had excellent language skills and a lot of experience in very specialized legal work. For them, I felt it might be a better option to market themselves as "bilingual legal consultants" or look for work directly with law firms rather than working their way up the agency ladder.

1.7 Finding your first translation clients

I receive a lot of inquiries from people who would like to become translators, and most of these e-mails have something to do with finding those first few elusive translation clients. If you ask 100 translators how they got started in the business, you'll probably get at least 50 different answers. Some picked up the phone and started cold-calling, some turned an old business connection into a client, some volunteered, some went back to school, some were just in the right place at the right time. Following are some tips on how to break into the translation industry, depending on your interests and level of experience.

As a freelance translator, your two basic categories of clients are translation agencies (companies that serve as a middleman between an end client and various freelance translators) and direct clients, where you work directly for the translation buyer with no middleman involved. Each of these approaches has its benefits and costs; translation agencies can sometimes provide a steady flow of work to their regular translators and provide value-added services such as marketing, collections, proofreading and project management, but in return for this, the agency takes a portion of the total fee they collect for the translation. Direct clients can offer higher earning potential, but often require the translator to perform additional tasks such as quoting jobs, editing, proofreading, collections etc. that are usually handled by agencies.

If you're starting out by applying to translation agencies, remember to play by their rules in order to maximize your chances of getting work. Most agencies have a translator application form on their websites; the "Contact Us" or "Opportunities" sections of agency websites are good places to look for these. Although it feels impersonal to apply for work this way, resist the urge to distinguish yourself by sending in a paper resumé if the agency requests an electronic one; what seems to you like a personal touch will only create more work for your potential client, and may get your application materials tossed without a second look. Along the same lines, most agencies prefer not to be contacted by phone unless you are applying for a specific position that they've advertised. If the online application form includes a "Comments" field, this is the place to ask for an in-person meeting or introduce yourself as a new translator in the area.

Whether applying to translation agencies or direct clients, there are a few basic rules to follow. You're applying for language work, so your application materials should be error-free. Make sure that everything you send out is proofed by yourself and at least one other person. When sending inquiries by e-mail, use a clear subject line, such as "German-English freelance inquiry." Don't disguise your intentions or make your message look like a response to an e-mail from the agency. State your language pairs prominently. As amazing as it may sound, many people neglect this simple step. Start your e-mail with a sentence such as "I am a freelance English to Spanish translator and I would like to offer my services to your agency/company, etc."

Use translation industry directories wisely. Translators associations and translation client rating lists are great places to find the names of agencies to apply to, but make sure not to misuse or abuse these resources. For example, once you find an agency in a translators association directory, never (never!) use the contact information that is listed in the directory. Simply go to that agency's website and follow the application process listed there.

Looking for work with direct clients has some positive and negative points for a beginning translator. As a newcomer to the profession, it can be helpful to have some of the safety nets that a translation agency offers; for example when you work for an agency, your work is almost always proofread before being sent to the end client, which guards against a true disaster if you make a mistake. However, direct clients, especially those located in areas where there are not many translators to choose from, may be more likely than a translation agency to take a chance on an inexperienced translator. Whereas a translation agency has a wide range of translators to choose from with no geographic restrictions, a direct client who wants to work with someone local has a bigger incentive to work with someone new.

If you'd like to work with direct clients, any large businesses, hospitals or school systems in your area are worth contacting, even if they don't have obvious international ties. Probably the best source of direct client contacts is international business organizations such as international chambers of commerce since you can be sure that the member companies use your non-English language in their business operations. Joining one of these organizations is also an excellent way to network with potential clients. Try Googling the chamber of commerce for the home countries of your language pair, i.e. "German-American Chamber of Commerce," "Korean-American Chamber of Commerce," etc.

Think locally. Especially if you present yourself better in person than on paper, start out by asking for in-person meetings with every translation or interpreting agency in your local area. By asking for a meeting to learn more about the agency and talk about how you might fit in, you'll both benefit from the interaction. Don't be dissuaded if local agencies "have no work in your language combinations right now." By asking for an in-person meeting, you'll position yourself to step in when their needs change.

Blanket the field. One of the biggest mistakes made by beginning translators and interpreters is to assume that they will be working full-time after sending out five or ten inquiries. On the contrary, you should expect no more than a one percent return rate on your cold-contacting efforts. A good start (emphasis: start) if you'd like to be working full-time would be to contact 300-500 potential clients during your first year in business. Your prospective clients may include translation agencies in the U.S., agencies in countries where your other languages are spoken, and companies in your area that could use your services.

Keep in touch. Instead of just firing off e-mails or making phone calls and then waiting to hear back from your potential clients, keep a log of the person you talked to or e-mailed and what his or her response was to your inquiry. As you get more experience, periodically contact these people to let them know that you're still interested and available. Let them know what types of projects you've been working on, and let them know that you would be happy to help them out with similar jobs.

Once you've landed your first few clients, marketing yourself becomes easier in the sense that you have something to tell new prospective clients about, other than the fact that you're looking for work. In general, even a successful freelancer must spend at least ten percent of his or her time on marketing; for beginning translators this figure may increase to as much as 50 percent, and for those who have been in the business for many years, the need to market may fall by the wayside. However, many marketing experts caution that "if you're not marketing, you're dying." While this advice may seem extreme, it's important for even experienced translators to prepare for the loss of a major client or a downturn in the economy by keeping up a steady flow of outbound promotion.

1.8 Freelance translation FAQ

I love to read lists of Frequently Asked Questions (FAQs) on topics that interest me, so I thought that I would periodically post some freelance translation FAQs. The questions are based on my experience and opinions and those of translators I've worked with and taught.

- Q: Do I need a Bachelor's degree to be a translator?

- A: Yes. No. Maybe. Parade Magazine incurred the wrath of many freelance translators when it rated translation as the #2 hot job with "no college degree required." While there are definitely jobs for translators that don't absolutely require a college degree (for example, some U.S. government agencies base their hiring exclusively on their own testing programs), it's very rare to meet a successful freelance translator who doesn't have at least a Bachelor's (I personally don't know any), and quite frequently a Master's or higher.

- Q: Do I need a graduate degree to be a translator?

- A: It's not an absolute requirement, but it definitely helps. For example, a graduate degree helps you meet the eligibility requirements for the American Translators Association certification exam.

- Q: How much can I earn as a freelance translator?

- A: Of course, everyone's mileage varies, it depends on your skills, clients, motivation and many other factors. In general, the average self-employed full-time freelance translator in the U.S. earns approximately $75,000. My opinion, based on my business and those of other translators I work with, is that a translator with excellent language skills and assertive marketing techniques should be able to earn $70,000-$80,000 and still maintain a good quality of life. Six figures is definitely not out of the question if you are willing to work long hours or if you work in a high-demand language pair or specialization.

- Q: How long does it take to get established as a freelance translator?

- A: Here again, it really depends on your situation. I've met people who had a full-time business up and running in a few months, and people who have been at it for years and don't seem to have the ball rolling yet. Generally, I would allow six months to a year to get a full-time business up to speed. I started part-time, contacted 400+ (not a typo) potential clients during my first year in business and it took 18 months until I was replacing my income from my previous full-time job.

- Q: Do I have to be certified to work as a freelance translator?

- A: In the U.S., translator certification is managed by the American Translators Association and translator certification is not a requirement for setting up your own business.

In my experience, being ATA-certified helps give you legitimacy as a translator; I would call it a "plus" but not a "must." In addition, ATA certification is not offered in every language combination, and is not offered at all in language combinations that don't involve English (for example, French into German or Spanish into Portuguese). Becoming ATA-certified involves meeting eligibility requirements, passing the written test, doing continuing education and maintaining your ATA membership. Not to be negative, but to be realistic, it's worth mentioning that the pass rate is below 20%. I think that certification is well worth it and that being ATA-certified helps me stand out in a popular language combination. Others would disagree and say it's expensive and not necessary, so it's really a personal decision.

1.9 Some thoughts on test translations

Test translations, whereby a potential client, often a translation company, asks a translator to complete an "audition" translation for free before beginning work with the client, are a frequent subject of controversy in the industry. Translators wonder if they should complete unpaid translations, if they should set a limit on the length of test translations, if they should offer to provide samples of their work instead, or if clients will be reluctant to use them if they do not complete test translations. Clients understandably want to hire highly-skilled translators, and one element of this is often to give the translator a test that many other translators have taken, in order to compare the new translator's work with that of established and trusted translators. In rare cases, translators either suspect or have proof that unscrupulous clients have used "unpaid tests" as a way to get some translation work done for free, which adds to the atmosphere of distrust surrounding tests.

One of the most common questions surrounding test translations (from the translator's point of view) is "should I take unpaid tests?" In and of itself, this question doesn't provide enough information to ensure a reliable answer, since the answer depends on a variety of factors. How long is the unpaid test? Who is the client? Is the test a tryout for a specific project? How much does the translator need or want the work in question? All of these are important factors to consider when deciding whether the time investment in taking an unpaid test is a good one.

Interestingly, item D of the ATA Code of Professional Conduct and Business Practices for "employers or contractors of translators and/or interpreters" reads: "I will not require translators or interpreters to do unpaid work for the prospect of a paid assignment." Although I guess that there is some room for interpretation (so to speak!) here, i.e. what constitutes "requiring" work; is a test translation "unpaid work" or something else entirely, this clause seems to take a stance against unpaid test translations, at least when they are given by translation companies that are ATA members.

For translation companies, the alternatives to unpaid tests, such as paid tests or small paid assignments, are more expensive and more risky, unless they have vetted the translator's background and experience before administering the test. For an agency that receives many unsolicited resumés, it's much easier to have the next step in the application process be "if you're interested in working for us, complete this test and return it" (which is likely to weed out many candidates). Also, translation is not the only profession where unpaid testing, even if it's not referred to as such, occurs. Within the past few years, I've conducted my own "unpaid tests" on a primary care doctor and a financial planner, both of whom offered a complimentary half-hour consultation before I committed to using their services.

Ideally, translation companies should consider paid translation tests as a cost of doing business, in the same sense that they see recruiting, hiring and training their in-house employees as a cost of business. Barring that, I think that it makes sense for translators to set some guidelines on when and how they take unpaid tests. In my own case, I ask the potential client to confirm two things before I take an unpaid test: 1) that they currently have or anticipate having a need for additional translators in my language combination; I do not take unpaid tests for the purpose of being added to an agency's general pool; and 2) that my rates (and I provide a rate sheet) are within the range of rates that they pay for my language combination. If the agency cannot confirm these, I don't take the test; other translators at a different point in their careers may have a different opinion about this. In addition, I think that it makes sense to put a limit on the number of words that you will translate as an unpaid test; I think that half an hour's work (for me this would be 200 to 250 words) is a reasonable limit, but again this is a personal decision.

Yet another option is for the translator to offer the prospective client some samples of work that he/she has done in his/her areas of specialization. To me, this is a more reliable indicator of the quality of the translator's work and it also allows the agency to review a larger sample of the translator's work than it can by administering an unpaid test.

1.10 My favorite mistake

No, not the Sheryl Crow song, the Newsweek/Daily Beast Column. Maybe I just love reading about other people's mistakes, but the last-page "My Favorite Mistake" essay is my favorite part of the redesigned Newsweek. Written by famous people of various flavors, these columns just reinforce the fact that whether it's Madeleine Albright wearing her "three monkeys" pin for a meeting with Vladimir Putin, Ricki Lake doing online dating or Dennis Quaid using cocaine, we are, as my yoga teacher would say, all on the path.

This week's essay, by violinist Joshua Bell, particularly grabbed my attention. Although I'm not a rabid fan of Bell's music, he's the subject of one of my favorite newspaper articles ever, Gene Weingarten's Pulitzer Prize-winning "Pearls Before Breakfast," in which Weingarten chronicles Bell's incognito performance in the Washington DC subway at rush hour. Bell's "My Favorite Mistake" column tells the story of his first international violin competition performance, in which he flubbed the opening of his piece and decided to stop, apologize to the audience and start over rather than soldiering on through the performance. This got me thinking that we translators and interpreters, who by nature thrive on being right about everything, could also benefit from hauling our favorite mistakes out of the archives. Here's mine. I told this story during the "Smart Business" panel at the Boston ATA conference so it's not totally fresh, but this is its first time in writing!

I started freelancing in 2002, right after my daughter was born. I had a Master's in French and had done a translation internship, but I really had no clue about the conventions of the translation industry. Plus, I was very, very hungry for work because I knew that my goal of working from home to be with my daughter was completely dependent on my success as a freelancer: if I didn't make it, it was off to full-time daycare for her and off to a cubicle for me.

One of the first assignments that I received was from an agency, a very simple birth certificate translation, maybe 100 words total. I think that my minimum charge at the time was $30, and the agency didn't give me any special instructions, just asked me to "translate the birth certificate." So there I am at my computer, thinking that this is the easiest $30 I've ever made. I mean, for 100 words, why even put the translation in a Word document? Why not just type it into an e-mail to save the client some time dealing with the attachment. Obviously the missing link here is my lack of knowledge of the conventions of translating an official document: the big time investment isn't translating the 50 or 100 words, it's re-formatting the translation to look as much as possible like the original. So off I go, typing the translation into an e-mail and firing it off to the client, feeling really proud of myself (aren't I efficient?!).

I have to say that the client was fairly understanding; probably more understanding than I would have been had I been on the receiving end of that e-mail. In any case I think they paid me the $30 we had agreed on, which was more than generous on their part since they ended up hiring another translator to do the job. But when I think back on this Favorite Mistake, I think that it really helped me. Obviously I learned something about official document translation, but I also learned a few larger lessons:

- Knowing how to translate and knowing how to run a freelance business are completely different things; to succeed as a freelancer, you need to know both.

- Try as we might to forget it, we were all new, inexperienced freelancers once. Maybe someone else's stupid mistake wasn't quite as stupid as mine, but we've all made them.

- When translation newbies ask uninformed questions (Why doesn't my TM tool spit out a translation after I type something into it? How much do I have to pay to get work from an agency? I charge 2 cents a word, is that about the industry standard? I'm looking for a business that's easy to run in my spare time, would conference interpreting be good?), it's hard not to be condescending, but it's important to at least try. Whenever I answer a question like these, I think back to my "this is the easiest $30 I ever made!!" moment and try to give a thorough and non-condescending answer. Although these questions (and my birth certificate mistake) are completely off the mark, I also think it's fair to ask how someone who's never worked as a translator would know that TM and MT are two different things, or that agencies don't charge up-front fees, or that the highest-paid freelancers make 40 or 50 cents a word, or that conference interpreters go to school for years just to learn the basics of the job.

1.11 The ten essentials of freelance translation

There's something about the number 10. Not just the connotation of "perfect 10," but the number has an undeniable appeal. This year's American Translators Association Translation Company Division conference was focused on the number 10 (10 sessions that each featured 10 tips on a certain topic), and people really seemed to enjoy the manageable scale of the presentations.

In my non-translation life I spend a lot of time in the mountains, so I've long abided by the guideline of The Ten Essentials that everyone should take into the backcountry. Outdoor enthusiasts are advised to equip themselves with a map, compass, sun protection, food/water, extra clothes, headlamp, first aid kit, fire starter, matches and a knife. This got me thinking about The Ten Essentials as applied to other areas of life, specifically freelance translation. What 10 must-have items would you recommend that every freelance translator arm herself or himself with? I'll go with (in no particular order):

1. Business cards; the kind without a "Get your free business cards at..." imprint on the back

2. A reliable computer

3. A computer backup system and potentially a backup computer

4. A good office chair, yoga ball or treadmill desk

5. A separate business bank account to keep business and personal finances separate

6. A membership in at least one association for professional translators

7. A high-quality computer keyboard; it sounds like a minor thing, but it's important when you're tap-tap-tapping away at those keys for 30-50 hours a week!

8. A few good dictionaries in various flavors; print, online, general, specialized, etc.

9. A thesaurus; some days I use mine more than my French-English resources. For those times when you just need another way to say it!

10. At least one trusted colleague. I realize these aren't available at Office Max, but I do think it's hard to reach your full freelance potential without a good network of colleagues.

2 Growing your freelance business

2.1 The importance of aiming low

... well, maybe not "low." Maybe "The importance of setting realistic expectations" is a better way to put it.

Over the years, I've noticed that many translators fail to reach their long-term goals because (paradoxically) they aim too high. Typical case scenario: a translator who has been in the business for a few years wants to move into the direct client market. Instead of marketing to small consulting companies, other solo entrepreneurs or small professional associations, the translator targets Fortune 500-size companies and is disappointed in the lack of response. Following are some tips on how aiming low/setting realistic expectations can help you achieve your long-term professional goals.

- Break daunting tasks into smaller chunks. Sandra Smith, the multi-award-winning translator of *Suite Française* and many other titles, told me that she finished her first book-length translation by translating two pages every morning. This is a great strategy: rather than waiting for that big block of time that is never coming ("I'm waiting to translate this book because I need a month with nothing else to do"), pick a daily chunk of work that you will actually do.

- Stop waiting to be completely ready. I'm currently reading C.J. Hayden's *Get Clients Now*, and really loved her tip- "You will never be completely ready. Start from where you are." This relates to a post I wrote last year on the tyranny of the sub-goal. Don't let the elusive goal of complete readiness hold you back. If you're avoiding doing e-mail marketing because your website is out of date, go to some in-person networking events instead. If you feel like you need 100 prospects in order to market in a new specialization, find one prospect a day and contact each prospect as soon as you find them.

- Focus on building critical mass. Especially if your goals relate to marketing, focus on how many contacts you will have made if you persevere over time. One contact a day doesn't sound like much, but if you contact one potential client a day for three months, you will have made 60 contacts. And I'm guessing that if you wait until you have time to contact 60 potential clients at once, you will probably never get there.

- Aim at the appropriate level. Over time (and through a combination of success, failure, frustration and elation!) I've learned that in order to land a new client, you need to be able to get to the person who can actually hire you. Hence, in the Fortune 500 example at the start of the post, the translator likely failed because he/she did not have the level of contacts to get to the person who actually procures translation services for IBM or Sanofi-Aventis or the World Bank. But if you focus on organizations where you can make a direct contact with the person who can write a purchase order for your services, you'll be a lot more successful. Some freelancers are at the level of the aforementioned organizations and some are at the level of contacting small consulting firms. Either way, if you aim at the appropriate level, you'll get some interest!

- Aim in accordance with your personality. Case in point: I hate cold calling. I'm actually not a big phone person in general, even with my own friends. So I don't even think of cold-calling prospective clients. E-mail works if you do it correctly and really target your messages. In-person networking works, because you learn to ask people about themselves so that you don't have to talk about yourself so much. People love getting handwritten notes because it shows an investment of time and attention on the part of the person who wrote the note. So regardless of what you think of the potential effectiveness of a marketing technique, focus on what you will actually do and what will actually work for you.

2.2 Book review: The Entrepreneurial Linguist

I've been meaning to review Judy and Dagmar Jenner's book *The Entrepreneurial Linguist: The Business-School Approach to Freelance Translation* since before this fall's ATA conference... Fortunately I took notes when I read it over the summer, so here we go!

The Entrepreneurial Linguist is available from Lulu Press www. lulu.com for $25.00 (paper copy) or $17.00 (file download). Judy and Dagmar Jenner co-wrote the book, which includes illustrations by Alejandro Moreno-Ramos of the popular Mox's Blog www.mox.ingenierotraductor.com. Its 11 chapters cover business skills for intermediate to advanced freelance translators and the book's focus is on running a freelance translation business as a business rather than as a money-making hobby (excellent advice!).

I highly recommend this book, largely because it is light on theory and heavy on nuts and bolts tips that the reader can apply immediately. For example, the section on trade shows includes a checklist of ways to connect and follow up with potential clients who are trade show exhibitors. Likewise, the marketing chapter lists typical reasons why a translator might lose clients, and offers tips on how to avoid each of these reasons. As an added bonus, most of the chapters include business school-style case studies that illustrate how the book's concepts can be applied in real-life freelance business situations.

Some of my favorite sections of this book are:

- how to get the most out of professional conferences

- options for business phone service

- sample auto mileage spreadsheet

- ways to decrease your office expenses

- the above-mentioned section on using trade shows as a marketing tool

- specific advice about blogging for business, for example sample post topics

- sample press release and information about how to use press releases as a marketing tool

- how to make a basic professional website on a tight budget

Judy and Dagmar also do a great job of dispelling the negative and self-defeating ideas that many translators have about direct client marketing. In a great section called "Yes, you can!," they chip away at the typical marketing excuses that many translators make: I'm too busy, I already have enough work, direct clients are too demanding, I don't know where to start, etc. While emphasizing that finding well-paying direct clients is not easy, the authors prove that marketing to direct clients is mostly a matter of getting out of the translation industry, going where your potential clients are (online and in the real world) and positioning yourself as a trusted authority.

Although I've been in the translation industry for close to a decade and wrote a translation business book, I've found myself referring to *The Entrepreneurial Linguist* on a regular basis ever since I read it. Judy and Dagmar are staunch advocates of charging what you're worth, finding clients who value your work and giving your clients a very high-quality product: even experienced translators can't get too much of this message! The only points I found myself disagreeing with are Judy and Dagmar's selection of Facebook as the most valuable social networking site for freelance translators (I like it for personal use and I think it's great for event-based businesses but I'd use LinkedIn or Twitter for professional contacts) and the fact that the book doesn't have an index. However, the table of contents is very thorough and it's not hard to find the section you're looking for!

In conclusion, I would highly recommend *The Entrepreneurial Linguist* for freelancers at all levels, especially intermediate and advanced freelancers who are looking to move into the direct client market. Judy and Dagmar also have a great blog, Translation Times (`www.translationtimes.blogspot.com`), and you can follow them on Twitter (`www.twitter.com`) at language_news.

2.3 Review your professional association memberships

I owe many thanks to my friend and colleague Eve Bodeux (`www.bodeuxinternational.com`) for suggesting this timely post! At the start of the new year, you probably receive membership renewal notices from the professional associations to which you belong. You may also be receiving solicitations to join new associations. Following are some tips on deciding whether to renew (or not), join (or not) or invest your time (or not) in professional associations.

First, there may be an objective reason to renew some of your memberships. For example, if you are ATA-certified, you are required to maintain your ATA membership in order to use the Certified Translator credential. If you belong to any associations that have a similar policy, or that charge a late fee if you do not renew on time, pay those dues first.

Then, you might want to look at whether you made the most of your association memberships during the previous year. For example, many associations allow non-members to attend their events by paying a higher fee. Did you attend enough events to recoup your membership dues investment, or would you be better off letting your membership lapse and paying the non-member fee? Is the association's e-mail list particularly valuable? If you joined the association for networking purposes, did you actually land some translation projects through your contacts?

To avoid redundancy, research whether you are a member of

any associations through an association you already belong to. For example, Colorado Translators Association purchases a yearly institutional membership to the Denver World Trade Center, so our members can attend WTC events at the member price. Likewise, FIT, the International Federation of Translators, allows members of its member associations such as ATA to attend its events.

And a few pieces of unsolicited advice:

- Be selective about how many event-based associations you join. For example, there are several great event-based professional associations in Denver that I could benefit from joining. However, when I look realistically at how many of those events I will actually attend, membership looks less attractive.

- Consider joining the translators' association in your non-English language country if they'll take you as a member. Especially if these associations have active e-mail lists, they can be excellent networking venues because you, as a US-based translator, are a rare commodity!

- Try to belong to at least one association related to your specialization(s). This does not have to be expensive; I recently joined the Society for International Development for 35 euros per year.

2.4 My favorite non-translation business books

A little note before we get started: none of the links in this post are affiliate links, nor do I get a commission from any of the authors mentioned. I love reading (and writing!) books about translation; some of my new and recent favorites are Chris Durban's *The Prosperous Translator* and Judy and Dagmar Jenner's *The Entrepreneurial Linguist*. I really enjoy getting insider tips from people who do the same job that I do, and I think that no matter how long one has been in the business, books like these always have some great suggestions for improvement!

I also think that getting perspectives from outside the translation industry is really important. For example, I think that lots of translators spend most or all of their networking time hanging out with other translators and translation company owners, then complain that they cannot find any direct clients. Reading some non-translation business books is a good first step in expanding your perspective. I'll give you a few of my favorites and I'm sure that some readers have other suggestions!

- C.J. Hayden's *Get Clients Now* is one of my top picks. It's an ultra-practical guide for freelancers and consultants of all flavors. The book helps you analyze where in the sales and marketing cycle you are stuck. Do you not have enough prospective clients? Do you get lots of inquiries but too few sales? Do you have lots of one-time clients and too few regulars?, etc. You then pick two or three major marketing projects that you want to work on, and ten daily actions that will help you complete those projects. For example, I purchased Hayden's book a few months ago when I decided that I absolutely had to finish the second edition of my book and get Eve Bodeux's and my webinar series off the ground. I identified some daily actions such as planning ahead for every day, doing half an hour of research three times a week, spending half an hour a day on the webinar series website, identifying two potential sales channels for the book every day, and so on. And hey, one of my major projects is completed and the other is almost there! This book will appeal to people who like concrete action plans and are good at executing them; definitely indispensable if you have a major marketing goal you want to achieve. Just for the record, the second edition of my book had been hanging over my head for two years, and I finally finished it with the help of this book.

- John Kremer's *1001 Ways to Market Your Books* was my bible when I published the first edition of my book: I've written this thing, now I need some people to read it! With about 700 pages (seriously) of tips, there is something for every self-published author in this book. Kremer breaks his ideas down into manageable chunks: how to write a book that people want to read, how to market it online, how to sell to libraries as a self-published author, and so on. With 1001 ideas, obviously not all of them will appeal to everyone, but this book is a fantastic resource.

- During my "aspiring freelancer" days, one of my first business reads was Peter Bowerman's *The Well-Fed Writer*, and I also really like his new book *The Well-Fed Self-Publisher*. I don't agree with all of Bowerman's advice. He's a huge proponent of cold-calling and I think it just doesn't fit with most translators' personalities or those of our clients, but I love Bowerman's "If I can do it, you can do it" attitude and his emphasis on simple, repeatable actions that you integrate into your marketing plan. In addition, Bowerman gets big points for his willingness to share his own examples: he started out as a salesman for a video dating service (seriously) and repackaged himself as a six-figure copywriter within a few years. He also really advocates charging high rates for your services and setting high but achievable income goals. Excellent inspiration here, and his book on self-publishing is well worth a read if you're an author.

2.5 Tips for a successful translation conference presentation

Here in Colorado, excitement about the Denver ATA conference is reaching a fever pitch and I'm spending today putting the finishing touches on my preconference seminar, "Beyond the Basics of Freelancing." I've read a number of good posts about how to get the most out of a translation conference, so here are a few tips on how to deliver an effective presentation! In my experience, presenting at an ATA conference or another translation industry conference is a great way to increase your name recognition, share your knowledge and force yourself to learn about some new topics; give it a try!

- Pick a topic with which you feel very comfortable. At a conference with 1,500 attendees, there will be experts in the audience, so you should be one too!

- Prepare, prepare, prepare. There are gifted public speakers and adequate public speakers, but it's excruciating to watch a speaker who's fumbling through papers, trying to ad-lib without much success or doesn't really know which slide is coming next. The first few times I presented at an ATA conference I wrote out a script with nearly every word I was going to say, and I still do this when I present in French.

- Don't be afraid to run the show; after all, you're the presenter! I used to be more flexible about answering questions during the presentation, but I found that it was easy to become bogged down in the process. Now I ask people to hold their questions unless they are purely factual, i.e. "what does CAT stand for."

- Repeat the questions. This is something that's hard to remember to do because it's not instinctive. Yet it's extremely frustrating to be sitting in the back of a large conference room while the speaker carries on an energetic dialogue with someone you can't hear.

- Engrave the presentation's ending time on your wrist. OK, it's a small exaggeration, but when you're nervous it's very hard to remember how much time you have left. If I'm giving a long seminar, I write BREAK on the notes for the slide before the break, and I do actually set an alarm for the session's end time!

- Give your audience a way to contact you. I leave a large stack of my inexpensive business cards out on a table at the front of the room. I try not to promise to answer individual questions, but I do answer some questions on my blog.

Also, I will say that as a speaker, it's incredibly gratifying to get e-mails from people who enjoyed a presentation. After the ATA conference, think about writing two or three quick e-mails to the presenters whose presentations you really enjoyed.

2.6 Some thoughts on setting goals

Goal-setting is a critical element of running a freelance business, but many translators ignore it. Not surprisingly, this type of passive attitude can lead to job stress and low job satisfaction, because instead of feeling that you're actively progressing toward your ideal freelance business, you feel like your clients are dictating how, when and at what rates you work. Here are some suggestions for active goal-setting:

- Rank your clients. I think of my clients as A, B or C level, you can come up with your own categories.

- A clients are what you might call "drop everything" clients; they pay well, they're easy to work with and they have interesting projects. The catch with A clients is that they may not need your services regularly, so unless you have a lot of them, you need another income base.

- B clients are the foundation of your business. These clients pay fairly and on time and fill your inbox with work, which is sometimes interesting and sometimes tedious. In my case, my two biggest B clients provide about 60% of my income.

- C clients are clients with whom you work only when you have some external motivation; business has been slow, they offer an especially interesting project. etc.

Once you have ranked your clients, think about how you can find more clients at the A level. Identify specific characteristics of your A clients, and search around the web for more potential clients like them. This will also reveal some characteristics of your business, which is an additional benefit. For example, once a translator reaches a certain level in the profession, A level clients are increasingly going to be direct clients, because the translator will move beyond an agency's maximum rates. A translator who has reached that level cannot increase his/her income without making the jump to working with more direct clients.

- Inventory your likes and dislikes. Be honest with yourself about what you like and dislike about being a freelance translator. Do you enjoy the work but find your current specializations boring? Do you love the flexibility but hate the stress of rush projects? Then, find some ways to shift your work toward the aspects of it that you enjoy. This type of inventory is part of what led me to switch to a treadmill desk, once I realized that one of my main "dislikes" was sitting at a desk all day.

- Set some specific, achievable goals. I think that these two characteristics, specific and achievable, are what make goals worthwhile. Instead of something amorphous like "make more money and be less stressed about work," force yourself to come up with some measurable objectives that you feel you can reach. This could be finding two new direct clients that pay more than X cents per word within the next six months, or finding at least one new client that works in a specialization you want to pursue, or not working more than one night per week, or increasing your income by 25%, or any other concrete goal that you feel will help your business.

2.7 When to seek professional help

We translators often complain that our clients don't understand the value of what we do: they expect us to work for minimum wage, they think that anyone who took a semester of college English can do what we do, they don't understand why it takes time to produce a good translation, and on and on. At the same time, I think that we're guilty of the same crimes when it comes to our use of other professional service providers: who needs a graphic designer/web copywriter/marketing consultant/public speaking coach? They're just going to rip me off! I'll save time and money and do it myself and the result will be fine! Except...the result is often sub-par. It seems to me that many translators (alas, including myself!) enthusiastically beat the "value of using a professional" drum when we're the ones who stand to gain from it; when we're the ones writing the check, we often turn to the equivalent of letting the bilingual mail room clerk translate the company annual report. Here are some areas in which I think translators could use some professional help:

- Web design. There's a big difference between a website that has the information you're looking for but is dated and tired-looking and a website that really makes you want to hang around for a while. One of my favorite freelancer websites is EN>FR translator Celine Graciet's (www.nakedtranslations. com). It's pretty, it's clean, it's easy to navigate. In an industry where so many of our business contacts come via the web, it's easy to see the business case for having a professionally-designed website.

- Copywriting. Even though we're all writers at heart, we're not all good marketing writers and it's very hard to write a good marketing pitch for your own business. FR>EN translator Sara Freitas wrote about this (in French) in her blog post (www.sfmtraduction.com/marmite/?p=299) about redoing her professional website. Sara writes that using a professional copywriter helped her create copy that speaks to her clients in their language, rather than remaining stuck in the language that translators use to describe our own businesses.

- Graphic design. Most translators have no unified visual identity whatsoever for their business. Or, their visual identity is either a piece of free clip art or whatever logo came with their web design package. A good visual identity can create a reminder of your business that spans your website, business cards, marketing materials, etc. and it doesn't have to be splashy. I really like Judy and Dagmar Jenner's twin girls holding hands (`www.twintranslations.com`) (for twins who translate together) and Karen Tkaczyk's atomic models filling in the letter M (`www.mcmillantranslation.com`) (for a chemical translator). A good graphic designer can really help with this.

- Marketing and pricing. Most of us know how to market to translation agencies, but many of us remain stuck there because we don't know how to market to direct clients. Many translators also struggle with negotiating rates and other terms of service. In addition, very few translators are good at networking out of the translation industry, for example by attending trade shows or conferences for professionals in their areas of specialization. A marketing or business development coach is someone who thrives on these aspects of business (which most translators dread!).

- A few others: How about a public speaking coach to help you deliver more effective presentations? A customer satisfaction researcher to interview your clients about your work? A really good accountant and financial planner to help you decide whether to incorporate and how to maximize your tax savings? An office designer to help you plan an appealing and functional workspace?

2.8 Break on through

In the past month I've been contacted by several translators who are at what I think of as the "make or break" phase of freelancing. They have a fair amount of work and their clients seem pleased with their translations, but they are not yet at the level of income and work volume where they would like to be for the long term.

In this situation, I think it's important to look at a few factors in order to break through to financial sustainability, and the point in your freelance career where you are spending your time working rather than looking for work. For example:

Have you allowed sufficient time to reach your goals? I would say that the average translator's startup phase could last from six months to a year, but that it's not unusual for many people to require two to three years to reach "cruising speed," where the freelance business becomes like a full-time job where you control the hours. Expecting this to happen after three or four months is, in my opinion, very optimistic.

Have you met the requirements of every project you have done? If you meet (or better yet, beat) your deadlines and deliver quality work that has been carefully researched and proofread, your clients will use you again. If you are lax about deadlines, don't allow time to ask terminology questions and proofread your work, it's time to tighten up your quality assurance system.

Are you targeting clients who have ongoing work? Sometimes, a client is very happy with your work but simply does not have a need for your language/specialization/etc. more than a few times a year. In this case, ask the client for a testimonial and use it to market your services to other clients.

Are you asking your clients for feedback? It's important to remember that a) some clients are not eager to give you constructive/negative feedback and that's their prerogative and b) a translation project manager's job does not necessarily include evaluating translators. That being said, it's worth asking your clients what you could do to better meet their needs, if they have any feedback on your services. etc. At the very least, this lets the client know that you are eager to improve and to work with them again.

Are you charging too much or too little? The rest of this blog's lifetime could be spent talking about rates, but in general, you want to avoid pricing yourself substantially above or below the market rates for your language pair. Charge too little and you'll mark yourself as either an amateur or someone who is not confident about your skills; charge too much and your clients will look elsewhere.

Are you targeting clients who fit your niche? In general, large agencies seem to prefer translators who work in a variety of specializations, charge moderate rates and can turn around large volumes of text in a short amount of time. In exchange, a large agency might be able to keep a translator busy close to full time. Smaller, boutique-style agencies often prefer specialized translators who, often in exchange for higher pay, are very meticulous about their work and don't mind answering questions about their terminology choices, target language phraseology, etc. Just make sure that you are targeting clients who fit your own work style.

Have you considered taking on a supplemental job? You've come this far; rather than abandoning your freelance business (assuming you enjoy it!), consider working at a bookstore or library, teaching language courses, doing tutoring, applying as an FBI contract linguist or another similar job that will help you keep your business afloat while you reach profitability.

3 Translation technique and translation quality

3.1 Which English?

Rumor, or should we say rumour, has it that many (or at least more than usual) translators on this side of the Atlantic are being approached to translate into what we commonly refer to here as U.K. English. I would guess that this has more to do with the falling U.S. dollar and weakening U.S. economy than with a sudden shortage of qualified into-English translators in the U.K.

This brings up a number of interesting questions. The first is, what is meant by U.K. English? Does this mean that the translator simply sets her/his spell-checker to U.K. English and uses U.K. date formats? Or does the translator attempt to write with a British flair, substituting "pudding" for "dessert" and "chemist's" for "pharmacy," or "at weekends" for "on the weekend"? A more conceptual issue is whether some sort of culturally neutral English is possible or desirable, and whether translation consumers are satisfied with translations that may be technically correct but stylistically more American than British.

According to U.S.-based German to English translator Jill Sommer, "Translating into U.K. English involves more than switching a z to an s. When a client contacts me for a U.K. English translation, I turn it down." Jill sees part of the problem as client misunderstanding of the many differences between U.K. and U.S. English and relates the story of a U.S.-based colleague who was asked, halfway into a 100+ page translation to "make it U.K. English." "At a minimum, clients should be willing to use a U.K. English proofreader. They underestimate the differences that make a text sound British or American," says Jill.

With session proposals for the ATA conference due soon, it seems like there might also be a niche for some linguistic education on this topic. Maybe a session on "Fundamentals of U.K. English for U.S. English translators" or "English with a British flair"? I would also be interested to know whether the reverse phenomenon happens on the other side of the Atlantic; do U.K.-based translation buyers automatically use U.S.-based translators, or do they ask U.K-based translators to Americanize their translations?

3.2 Keeping up your source language skills

Many translators insist that talking to anyone (clients, potential clients, colleagues, beginning translators, etc.) is unnecessary and detracts from their true calling, which can only be fulfilled by spending at least 10 hours a day at the computer. While that's somewhat of a joke, I think that many translators do feel that unlike interpreters, they don't really need to keep up their active language skills in their source language(s), and that passive (i.e. understanding what you read or hear) skills will suffice. In my experience, especially when dealing with higher-paying direct clients, it's actually quite important to be able to communicate fluently in your source language(s). Direct clients in particular are, I think, more inclined to use translators with whom they communicate well, whether it's over e-mail or on the phone, and are also more likely (whether for good reason or not) to mistrust a translator who has difficulty communicating in the client's language.

Obviously, many translators have a comparatively easy time keeping up their source language skills because they live all or part of the time in a country or community where their source language is spoken, marry someone who is a native speaker of their source language, use their source language in their non-work life, etc. However, many of us, and I'll include myself in this, have more logistical barriers to overcome. Taking myself as an example, my foundation in written and spoken French is strong, and I've spent quite a bit of time going to school, living and traveling in French-speaking countries. However, French is not widely spoken where I live, nor does anyone in my family speak French, nor do I, as the parent of a young family, visit French-speaking countries anywhere near as frequently as I did until a few years ago.

Once I realized that being able to maintain my written, spoken and cultural skills in French was essential to my business, I decided it was worth an investment of my time and money, and I think that this applies to other translators as well. I think that "linguistically isolated" translators have a number of options for keeping up their source language fluency: with the prevalence of online resources such as podcasts, blogs, online editions of newspapers, etc., it's quite easy to find free, high-quality materials in your source language. In addition, organizations such as the Alliance Française and the Goethe-Institut sometimes have classes that are suitable for advanced speakers. Many college and university towns also have foreign language conversation groups that welcome people at a variety of levels.

One resource that I've used over the years is the audio magazines from the now-defunct Champs Elysées; these were monthly publications for French, Italian, German and Spanish and were intended for "intermediate to advanced" language learners. Back issues may be available from your library, or you can take advantage of similar resources online by listening to podcasts, YouTube videos etc. in your source language.

3.3 Translators and proofreading: a love/hate relationship

Recently, the Colorado Translators Association held a great workshop with local editor and editing instructor Alice Levine. This session was really enlightening in a number of ways; Alice is a lively and engaging presenter and she seemed to enjoy speaking to a group of fellow "word geeks," and it also made me realize that translators and proofreading have a complex relationship that isn't easily resolved in the conditions under which most of us work.

Alice talked a bit about "the proofreading mindset," and how it's important to get into the right frame of mind when you're proofreading; right here, I realized why proofreading is one of the aspects of translation that I really have to work on. If I'm going to yoga three times a week, my mind is more in the mood to proofread; otherwise (and here I mean most of the time), I'm one of those people who naturally reads too fast, talks too fast, etc. and I think that many other translators fall into this category as well. At the same time, I, along with probably most other translators, have a very low error tolerance when it comes to the written word. A couple of days ago I was bothered for an inordinate amount of time over the fact that when taking my daughter to swimming lessons, I had to sign a paper saying, among other things, that she would not wear a swimsuit equipped with "flotation devises" [sic]. So, it's a tightrope that we as translators walk; we want our own work to be error-free, we're intensely bothered by errors in other people's work, yet most of us don't or can't do what it takes to produce perfect work.

To start out with, Alice advised our group that it's almost impossible to proofread well if you proofread on your computer screen, proofread your own work, proofread when you're tired, or proofread something without allowing a break of at least several hours between when you write/translate it and when you proofread it. Right there, you can see a variety of stumbling blocks that are just the nature of our jobs as translators. Often, printing hard copies of the documents we work on isn't practical because of length, or because we want to keep the translation in a translation environment tool until after it's been proofed. The reality of most of our specializations is that deadlines are tight; there often isn't time for a proofreader to go over the document and send it back to the translator for approval. Because of these tight deadlines, there is often barely enough time to finish a quality translation, much less allow a few hours' break before going back and proofing it two or three times.

At the risk of sounding like it's all gloom and doom, Alice's workshop definitely helped me come up with some techniques that I feel are realistic for myself and for other translators who work under deadline and who proofread on the computer screen. First, I think it's absolutely necessary to edit the target file against the source file once, then just read the target file on its own. When I do this, it amazes me how many errors I catch when I'm looking just at the target file. Alice emphasized the importance of realizing the limitations of the spell-checker, and she advised doing a search for homonyms such as too/to, their/they're, etc., which I think is also doable. Along those lines, whenever I'm working on a translation where I find myself confusing two terms that are similar (such as agent/representative, loan/credit, contract/agreement etc.), I do a search for just those words so that I can individually compare each word in the target document to the corresponding word in the source document.

Part of this goes back to my previous post on being paid by the word versus by the hour, or maybe this just relates to rates in general. In some sense, I think that being paid by the word discourages careful proofreading, because every time you go back over a word, you're effectively decreasing your hourly rate, whereas if you're paid by the hour, you're essentially rewarded for doing two, three or more very careful revisions of a document. In essence, this is what I think is at work in some environments such as high-level governmental and international organizations where translators may be expected to translate as few as 1,500 words a day because of the unending emphasis on quality. For those of us who work largely with the private sector, the speed versus quality equation is one that requires careful balancing. Alice's workshop was a really enlightening chance to reflect on how all of these factors affect translators' work and how we can improve quality within the parameters of our clients' needs.

3.4 Some thoughts on gender-neutral language

It's interesting how some linguistic issues seem to get solved and then are up for solution again, as seems to be the case with gendered pronouns in English. The first wave of gender-neutral language was inspired by the realization that many professions that had traditionally been all male (fireman, mailman) were now becoming more gender integrated, giving rise to terms like firefighter and mail carrier. Likewise, we realized that the default "he" might rub half the population the wrong way, and the proposed solution was to always include both genders, like "Every student should bring his/her own calculator."

As gender-neutral language has evolved, he/she has fallen out of favor and been deemed clunky, and a few alternatives are floating around. The easiest end-run around the he/she issue is to pluralize the subject and use "they" or "their," as in "Translators must bring their own dictionaries to the exam," "When students go on field trips, they must wear sneakers," except in situations where the subject clearly refers to one gender or the other, as in "Every egg donor receives compensation for her time."

On the other side of the coin, we sometimes need a new term when the habitual gender of the person who holds a certain role changes. The term "maestra" is seeing more exposure as the number of women orchestra conductors increases, and the U.S. now has a number of "First Gentlemen," the husbands of women governors.

It goes without saying that translation adds a whole other layer of mystique to the gender issue, especially since many of us work between English and a language that makes much more liberal use of gendered words. In French, you just can't get around the issue that a table is feminine and a book is masculine, but at least they both become "the" in translation; on the other hand, French doesn't have different words for his and hers, but instead uses *son/sa/ses* for both, which puts the issue in the translator's lap when those words are translated. French, and other languages like it, also have the interesting issue of words that are always masculine or feminine no matter who they refer to. I have to admit that it cracks me up to see French male movie stars referred to as *une vedette*, (a star), where they're not only feminine but get an "ette" to boot.

However, this too may be changing. Last month's issue of the French audiomagazine Champs Elysées featured an interview with Roselyne Bachelot, the (female) French Minister of Health, Youth and Sport, in which she responded to the interviewer's first question: *Madame la ministre ou Madame le ministre, Roselyne Bachelot?* by saying *On dit Madame la ministre, parce que c'est un mot épicène, qui suppose la possibilité de le mettre au féminin ou au masculin, comme secrétaire ou d'autres.* (We say *Madame la ministre*, because it's an epicene word, which implies the possibility of making it feminine or masculine, like secretary or other words).

It's worth noting that Bachelot's assertion that *Madame la ministre* is just fine has been vigorously opposed by French academics, but who knows, maybe John Malkovich will one day be *un vedet*.

3.5 I feel like I've read this somewhere before

Last night I was working on a translation of a news article; there was a quote from an expert in the article, so I Googled it to see if the quote appeared in English somewhere on the web. Interestingly enough, what popped up was a translation of the entire article. Enter a dilemma, and one that has various ethical and financial gradations. In this situation, I was able to talk to my client on the phone and explain the situation; since the translation was a rush job and due in a few hours, we decided that I would simply go ahead and do the translation as if the online version didn't exist, but the situation is not always this clear. Following are a few *déjà lu* (already read!) experiences I've had and how I've handled them.

Situation: You find a translation of your document on the internet. Some people would argue that if the client isn't willing to spend a few minutes searching for an existing translation, it's not unfair to go ahead and translate the document and charge the client for it. Personally, I always alert the client in a situation like this and offer to stop translating and be paid only for what I've already done, because if the existing translation is high-quality, it seems like a waste of effort to produce another one.

Situation: You have previously translated a document that's very similar to what you're working on, but for another client. Here, I think that it's a case of "leveraging your previous work" and it's fair to charge the client your full rate. I've run into this situation with insurance contracts, where two different clients sent me two insurance contracts that were 90% similar because they were issued by the same company. My take on this: when you have your will written up, the attorney doesn't charge less because she already has boilerplate documents prepared. As long as the document was for another client, I don't see a problem with charging full price.

Situation: You have previously translated a document that's very similar to what you're working on, and it was for the same client. Here, I'm inclined to err on the side of honesty. I would probably explain the situation to the client and offer to charge by the hour for reviewing the new document and making the changes. I think it's a little greedy to ask a client to pay you for 8,000 words when they already paid you to translate 7,500 of the same words.

Situation: You're translating a corporate document, and the text, or something close to it, is already on the company's website. I think this issue can be argued from both sides. In one sense, the company should be checking that it doesn't already have a translation of what it's sending out. In another sense, if the document is sent out for translation, there may be a reason the company wants a new or different translation. I would probably verify with the client, but I don't think it's absolutely dishonest not to.

3.6 A little bit of this, a little bit of that

An excellent blog post by Gabe Bokor entitled "Specialist or Generalist" (translationjournal.blogspot.com/2008/07/specialist-or-generalist.html) gives some insights into the fact that translators often need to be both specialists and generalists. Gabe gives the example of a medical translator who also needs to be familiar with electronic instrumentation, or an environmental translation project that may also include subjects like chemistry and meteorology. I think that Gabe's point holds true for most translation specializations, and emphasizes the need for all of us to be well-informed about a range of topics that are seemingly unrelated to our stated specializations.

In the case of legal translation, high-level lawsuits are about laws. That's how you end up with the late Anna Nicole Smith at the Supreme Court. When Justice Ruth Bader Ginsburg wrote that opinion, the primary issue before the Court wasn't whether Anna Nicole was entitled to her late husband's vast fortune, but whether state probate courts have the authority to oversee wills and the execution of estates. In other words, a legal question.

However, lower-level lawsuits don't deal with the intricacies of the law so much as they deal with a specific factual question. Did the landlord know about the asbestos-laden tiles when he put the office building up for rent? Was the employee fired because she was a woman, or because she didn't produce results? Did the company increase its cash reserves to deliberately mislead investors? And how thick was the sheet metal on the hull of the ship that sank? So, although a legal translator certainly has to be familiar with legal terminology, the translator also learns something about a very wide range of topics along the way.

Likewise, patent translation deals partially with the terminology specific to patents, like inventive step and prior art and the European Patent Office Oppositions Division, but a patent is also about something, like a car part or a cancer drug or an ergonomic computer mouse. So, the "patent translator" may be what we would call highly specialized, someone who translates nothing but patents, while in reality the translator works in a new "specialization" nearly all the time.

To me, this aspect of translation work is one of the most interesting. Although about 60% of my work is discovery documents for corporate lawsuits, these lawsuits involve something different nearly every time. So, instead of feeling like "same old, same old," this variety keeps things fresh!

3.7 Some thoughts on translation specializations

One of the issues with which beginning translators frequently struggle is specializing: what to specialize in, how to decide what to specialize in, what the most/least requested specializations are, how important it is to specialize, etc. While there aren't too many hard and fast rules when it comes to translation specializations, here are a few general guidelines.

The larger the language, the greater the need to specialize. Here in the U.S., translators in smaller-diffusion languages like Finnish or Thai often don't need to specialize at all, because there are so few of them that specializing would be impractical. On the other hand, French, German and Spanish translators must specialize in order to find a niche in a rather large market.

Pick a specialization that you enjoy researching. This advice comes from Jill Sommer, who taught for many years in the graduate translation program at Kent State, and I agree completely. Think about picking up a news magazine; which section are you most likely to read first? Business? Finance? Health? Technology? Any area that you enjoy learning more about is a potential specialization. Realize that for better or for worse, many translators are self-taught in their specializations. Many people seem daunted by the idea of specializing, fearing that they need to go back to school and get a nursing degree to be a medical translator, or become a paralegal to be a legal translator. Certainly, many translators do have a strong background in their areas of specialization, and if you come into the field as a former financial analyst, physician or attorney, you are likely to command a higher income than a translator who learned that terminology on the job. But if you're entering the market with a general liberal arts background, don't be intimidated by the idea of selecting a specialization.

Oddly enough, specialization can lead to more work rather than less, as clients think of you as the go-to person for documents in your area of expertise. Also, as several people have commented on this blog, one way to make more money as a freelance translator is to work faster, and the better you know the terminology of the documents you work on, the faster you can translate.

While it's theoretically possible to specialize in almost anything (I've met translators specializing in horses, philately, and fisheries, to name a few), you'll probably want to pick an area that you know is in demand. A few such domains would be medicine, medical instrumentation, pharmaceuticals, law, finance, automotive, computer hardware and software, engineering, environmental science, patents, advertising, technology, the hard sciences and general business documents.

Consider delving deeper into a specialization that you enjoy. A great way to position yourself ahead of your competition is to take courses in the terminology of your specialization, or to spend a day at a place of business or an industrial facility that works in your specialization, then let your clients know about it!

4 The freelance mindset

4.1 Shoshin

This post has either nothing or everything to do with translation, depending on how you look at it! Here goes: I've been thinking a lot about Shoshin, the Zen Buddhist concept most commonly translated as "Beginner's Mind." It's most commonly described as an attitude of openness and lack of cynicism about experiences, or as the ability to see a familiar experience from the perspective of a beginner. At the same time, I had been looking for a goal to work toward for my upcoming 40th birthday. Long and expensive story short, I decided to combine my interest in teaching and my passion for telemark (free-heel) skiing and take a season-long ski instructor training course. The course is in progress right now, and I've definitely gleaned a few translation-related observations from it.

- All of us should be more patient with beginning translators who don't know anything about translation or the industry but are eager to learn. Being an enthusiastic beginner is really, really hard. It's much harder than being an apathetic beginner. An apathetic beginner doesn't really care about excelling, while an enthusiastic beginner does. During the run-up to my ski course, I had a thousand and one dumb questions: do I bring my own lunch or are we buying? do I need a notebook that fits in my coat pocket? are we skiing right away or is the first day in the classroom? and on and on. Enthusiastic beginners ask lots of questions that seem, dare I say it, stupid, to experienced professionals, but we need to be more willing to answer these questions without being condescending.

- I love translation overall, but there are also things about it that don't thrill me all the time. My intent with this ski instructor idea has never been to quit translating. I love translating too much and I probably couldn't afford to ski full time even if I wanted to! However, this process has shown me that in some ways, sitting at a computer for every moment of my work day is draining in a way that doing something active and social for eight hours is not. This has made me think about incorporating more social stimulation and non-computer time into my translation work.

- Being forced into a challenging situation is an outstanding way to grow. After eight years of translating in my current specializations, I feel pretty confident about my abilities nearly all the time; I can't say (and this is largely my own fault) that I feel stretched, pushed or out of my comfort zone on a typical work day. But the first time my ski instructor took our group to a really steep tree-covered slope and said "see you at the bottom," I was terrified and convinced that I would have to be helicoptered out, or that I would be woefully inadequate compared to the rest of the class. This was a great exercise in positive self-talk rather than the negative self-talk that we freelancers engage in so often. I had to consciously tell myself "You can do this. You have practiced these maneuvers lots of times. Just take it slowly and don't forget to breathe!" And at the bottom (Yes! I didn't have to be helicoptered out!), I was ecstatic. I was intimidated, but I did OK because I trusted that I had built up a foundation of skills to get down that slope in one piece. That made me realize that I need to deliberately take on some translation work that is more of a stretch and a challenge: not a "get me out of here on a helicopter" challenge, but a "you are ready for this" challenge.

- Even experts have a lot more to learn. This is true of skiing and it's true of translation. My ski instructor is, to put it mildly, an amazing skier to watch. But when we looked at the video footage of ourselves skiing, he saw just as much room for improvement in his skiing as in the students'. This is part of the thrill of translation too; you can always become a better writer or learn more about your subject areas or read the translations of people who are more skilled than you are, and that's a very inspirational thing.

4.2 Are bad habits a form of self-protection?

I recently came across a very interesting interview in which sports writer Bill Simmons interviewed New Yorker writer Malcolm Gladwell (sports.espn.go.com/espn/page2/story?page=simmons/060302). Both Simmons and Gladwell draw some interesting parallels between sports and the rest of life, but my favorite is Gladwell's take on why certain people (in this case athletes, but it could be translators) "don't work hard when it's in their best interest to do so."

Gladwell posits, and I'd agree, that failure caused by poor preparation is a way to insulate oneself from a more awful possibility: failure caused by a lack of ability. Gladwell applies this theory to golfers Tiger Woods (an obsessive preparer on the golf course, whatever his vices off the course!) and Phil Mickelson (who states that he didn't pick up a golf club for five weeks before a major tournament), saying "...it's really risky to work hard, because then if you fail you can no longer say that you failed because you didn't work hard. It's a form of self-protection. I swear that's why Mickelson has that almost absurdly calm demeanor. If he loses, he can always say: Well, I could have practiced more, and maybe next year I will and I'll win then. When Tiger loses, what does he tell himself? He worked as hard as he possibly could. He prepared like no one else in the game and he still lost. That has to be devastating..."

Let's apply this to the business of freelance translation. Hopefully you achieved some or even most of your goals for this year. But as for the goals you didn't achieve, did you fail because you didn't follow through or did you fail because you followed through and still fell short of the target? I'm with Gladwell on this one; it's a lot easier to tell yourself that you didn't meet your income goal because you didn't have time to do your marketing than it is to accept that you marketed and marketed and things didn't pan out. Therefore, it's a lot safer not to do the marketing so that you have that excuse in your back pocket.

So here's a resolution: whatever your business-related goals are, give yourself permission to really, really try to meet them. Rather than protecting yourself with the usual "not enough time," "too much else going on" types of excuses (I'm as guilty of these as the next translator!), give those goals your best, most honest and most thorough effort. Accept that you might not reach them, but try to drop the self-protecting excuses!

4.3 Getting things done

When asked why they failed at freelancing, many former free-lancers say that they simply couldn't deal with the unstructured nature of the freelance day and ended up working out/watching TV/cleaning the closets etc. instead of working. Succeeding as a freelancer (translator or any other freelance job) requires that you be able to meet tight deadlines with very little external su-pervision. So, how do you avoid becoming one of those people with really clean closets and an empty checkbook? Here are some time management strategies that I use on a daily basis, which can be tailored to your work style and personality. For what it's worth, my closets are very messy, but I've never missed a freelance deadline!

- Enjoy what you do. This seems obvious, but when you look forward to your work, the temptation to avoid it in favor of other things decreases, and the reverse is true as well.

- Use visual reminders of what you have to get done. When you sit down at the computer with no visual cues in front of you, it's all too easy to check e-mail at a leisurely pace, read the news, get that second cup of coffee...and by that time you've convinced yourself that there's nothing very pressing for you to do anyway. If you have a visual reminder of a task, whether it's a to-do list, post-it notes or pop-ups on your computer screen, it's much easier to force yourself to act on it.

- Don't interrupt your work to perform small tasks. For most people, momentum and uninterrupted work time are key to completing projects. When you remember that you need to send an invoice, follow up with a client, check if you received a wire transfer, etc., don't interrupt what you're doing to perform the task. Instead, record it on your prioritized to-do list (see below!).

- Use a prioritized to-do list. I force myself to do this because the low priority items ("look for other translation-related blogs; research possibility of work-related trip to France") are much more alluring than the high priority ones ("fill out W-2 forms; photocopy payroll taxes"). Although I'd much rather be doing the low priority items, having a category labeled "must be done today" makes me complete the high-priority tasks first.

- Keep a list of quick jobs where you can see it. I think it's very tempting to waste time in small increments, because you can ignore the fact that 10 minutes here and and there adds up to a lot of time over the course of a day or week, and it's not as if you just spent two hours trolling Craigslist. So, I keep out a list of jobs that take 5-10 minutes and aren't too oner-ous; entering business-related receipts into my accounting program, writing a check-in e-mail to a client, responding to a non-urgent e-mail that's descended to the bottom of my inbox, etc. and when I feel like taking a break from translating, I do one of those things.

- Give the day some structure. This depends on your work style, but I find that it's important to break the day in the home office up into chunks and set some goals for each chunk. For me, this avoids the "it's 4PM, where did the day go?" phenomenon.

- Take exercise breaks when you need to think. This might brand me as a resident of America's second fittest city, but I do think it works. When you have something you need to mull over, get out of the office and move instead of staring at the blank screen. If you want to be really productive about it, carry a digital voice recorder with you and talk into it while you exercise, then transcribe your thoughts when you get back to the office (refreshed!)

4.4 The art of saying no

Recently, several beginning freelance translators have asked me about how and when to say no to clients who are offering translation projects. It's a delicate topic, since as freelancers we need to accept work in order to stay in business, but we also need to decline work in order to maintain a good quality of life, and to avoid taking on projects that are outside our areas of expertise. Following are some tips on how to say no to clients without harming your future relationship with them.

When I decline a job because it is outside my area of expertise or because I think the deadline is unrealistic, I tell the client what the issue is, because I think that this builds an honest relationship with the the client, who is then more likely to believe me when I say that I can take something on. For example if the project involves very technical documents or hard science, I simply say, "It's not my specialization; the end result will be much better if you use a translator who specializes in that area." If the deadline is more than what I can take on, same plan of action: "I'm concerned that I can't do a quality job in that amount of time. Of course if you can extend the deadline..."

One advantage of this strategy is that I offer it as evidence to new clients. If the client seems nervous about using me and I want the project, I tell them that I regularly turn down work that is outside of my specializations, or I say "I never take on a project that I feel I can't do a good job on. I wouldn't give you a quote for this project if I weren't confident in my ability to produce a high-quality translation." This way, the client knows that I don't automatically say yes to everything.

Personally, I try not to refuse a project because of rate or deadline issues without at least putting forth a counter-offer. For example if a client says "we can pay X cents a word," where X is much lower than my rate, I might say "I would be very interested in this project if you can pay my base rate of Y cents a word." Depending on the situation, for example if I can tell that the client is new to purchasing translations, I might also suggest that "Of course you're welcome to look for someone who will work for that rate, but I would be concerned about quality since most established professional translators don't seem to be working for that rate." If the issue is deadline, I usually take a similar approach, "It sounds like a really interesting project, but I find that in order to produce a high-quality translation, I need to limit myself to 2,000-3,000 words per day. If you could give me 4 days to translate your 10,000 words, I would be happy to help out."

When you're weighing your decision on whether to accept a project, I think it's important to differentiate between a rush deadline and an unrealistic deadline. For better or worse, rush deadlines are the reality in many translation specializations. However, I think there's a difference between doing 10,000 words in three days (a real squeeze, but possible if you are very familiar with the subject matter and the documents are either in a read/write format or a very legible PDF and don't involve complex formatting) and doing (or more likely trying to do) 10,000 words in two days; at that level, I think it's almost impossible to work accurately enough that quality doesn't suffer.

I think it's also important to differentiate between going the extra mile/kilometer for your regular clients and allowing yourself to be exploited by new or infrequent clients who are in a bind. Not all translators share this view, but I feel that my regular clients deserve some special treatment for the quality of life that they allow me to enjoy, working on my own schedule, on interesting projects and earning a healthy income. So, if a regular client needs 10 words translated, I do it without charging. If a regular client's project requires a few hours of work on a weekend, I charge my regular rate instead of a premium rate. However, I don't do these favors for non-regular clients; the "royal treatment" is reserved for my top few (very few!) clients on whom my business depends. That's a post for another time, "The Art of Saying Yes!"

4.5 Twin Translations: A passion for languages, squared!

If you're a freelancer, chances are you've worked on "one of those projects" (or maybe more than one!) where you wished you had another one of you to take on some of the work. And if you're Judy or Dagy (short for Dagmar) Jenner of Las Vegas and Vienna-based Twin Translations (twintranslations.com), you picked up the phone, called the other one of you, and the problem was solved. Judy and Dagy, identical twins who grew up in Austria and Mexico before attending college in the U.S. (Judy) and Austria and France (Dagy), now work together as a translation company that never sleeps, offering translations from and into German, English and Spanish, with Dagy adding in some French.

I recently asked Judy and Dagy if they would be interested in being profiled for Thoughts on Translation (in the spirit of disclosure, Judy and I are friends, but I don't have any business associations with Twin Translations). Here's what they had to say!

Q: Are you two really twins? Or just really good friends?

A: We are definitely twins. Identical twins. Which means we pretty much look the same, talk the same, gesture the same way, like the same literature, music, things in life, etc. There are a few small differences, though. Dagy prefers vanilla ice cream and Judy is much more of a chocolate addict. Also, Judy goes for ketchup, Dagy goes for mustard. Dagy is Judy's younger sister, by 10 minutes.

Q: So where exactly are you from? Europe, Mexico, the US?

A: We are citizens of the world, in a way. We were born in northern Austria. At age 10, our dad got a job offer to run the Latin American operations for iron and steel division of his employer, which is now part of the German conglomerate Siemens. We moved there in 1987, and finished grade school and middle school at the German School of Mexico City. We moved back to Austria for our junior year in high school, and graduated there. After college, Judy took a full tennis scholarship to the University of Nevada Las Vegas, where she also received her M.B.A. in marketing. Dagy studied French and Communications at the University of Salzburg and in Tours, France, and afterwards studied Translation and Interpretation in Vienna, where she is currently getting her master's degree. Since college, we have been flying all over the world to see each other and spend time with our family. Dagy has been to Las Vegas, where Judy has lived since 1995, a total of 14 times. And it's the best day of the year every time we see each other at the airport. Dagy lives in Vienna, Austria, with her boyfriend and Judy's cat, who moved there from Vegas because Judy's husband is allergic to cats.

Q: Tell us a little about your language combinations.

A: Our active languages are German, English and Spanish. We both translate into all of these. Dagy also has a passive language, which is French, meaning that she translates from French into any of the other languages. Most clients ask us for translations from German into English and vice versa.

Q: What's your biggest translation pet peeve?

A: When a client asks for a free sample translation. While nobody would even consider going to an attorney and requesting a sample contract, people have no such qualms when it comes to translations. This is a professional service, and we are happy to provide future customers with references. And it also bothers us when clients tell us that they would've done the translation themselves if only they had had time. No wonder the world is full of awful translations (or translation attempts).

Q: What's the most challenging project you have translated during the last couple of years? A: One of the toughest projects was the translation of a technical brochure for Bösendorfer, an Austrian piano maker, from German into Spanish. It took us a while to understand how a piano works. We purchased a dictionary for piano terminology that also included pictures, which helped a lot. At that time, all we knew about pianos was that we had taken classes as kids and that we were awfully untalented. Now we know a lot more than that and that's the beauty of the job. Another challenging job was the translation of the huge web site of the Austrian Postal Service into English in merely two months. While Dagy translated during the day, Judy did the proofing at night.

Q: Do you have a sample of your favorite incorrect translation?

A: Too many to count, but here is one. A major translation company in the US outsourced a big Vegas-related translation project to dozens of freelancers who were not familiar with Vegas. Hence, the Las Vegas Strip (the main road where all the hotels are on) became „la franja de césped" (=the strip of grass). It never ceases to amaze us that large corporations, who hire the top attorneys, top CPAs, and the most highly trained software developers, want to save money on translation. The written word is every company's business card, and the translations also have to be top-notch if the company wants to be taken seriously in the country that it tries to do business in.

Q: So what language do you think in?

A: No idea. Another thing we don't know is what language we dream in. We're still trying to find out how to determine that.

Q: What language do you speak in with each other?

A: A wild combination of our common languages, German, Spanish, English. It's similar to the language that was spoken at the German School in Mexico City that we attended, but with a bunch of English thrown in because Judy is so Americanized now.

Q: Which fields do you specialize in?

A: Legal, business, technology, banking, marketing, etc. Lately, we've been doing a lot of music-related translations (they say Vienna is the world capital of music), logistics and a combination of legal and financial translations for the Austrian National Bank.

Q: What kinds of translations do you not do?

A: We are not licensed to do certified translations of birth certificates, etc.

4.6 Finding the time

Time management is an aspect of freelancing that many people struggle with. In one sense, a freelancer's time belongs to her or him, which is a beautiful thing. Rather than the rigidly controlled life of the office worker, a freelancer can make the 10-step commute from the bedroom to the office at 6AM, 10AM, noon or later and then work until the work is done, scheduling shopping, cooking, exercising or socializing as time allows.

At the same time, the amorphous structure of a freelancer's work day has its disadvantages. An office worker has an external incentive (let's call it "the boss") to get to work on time, put in an eight, nine or ten hour day and produce results. In addition, an office worker doesn't have to explain why he or she can't drop a friend's dog off at the vet or let the neighbor's plumber in, because the office worker has a strict boundary between home and office.

I think that there are a number of good productivity strategies that home-based translators can apply. A few of my favorites are:

- Use a prioritized to-do list or a day planner. When you're translating away and suddenly remember that you need to check on overdue invoices, pay your credit card bill or buy printer paper, don't stop what you're doing to perform that task. Instead, write the task on your list or in your planner, and do all of the small tasks at once during a work break.

- Realize that it's acceptable to be "at work" even though you're at home. Answer the home phone line sparingly; warn house guests that you will be working while they're visiting; don't feel obligated to be the person who's always free during the day just because you work at home.

- Do the "have to" tasks before the "want to" tasks. On your to-do list, list the tasks that must be done that day first; don't let yourself fiddle around with your website when you should be doing your payroll taxes.

- Give yourself a time frame for non-work tasks. One of the things I really enjoy about freelancing is the ability to do things like banking, grocery shopping or getting the car's oil changed at off-peak times, but I make sure to give these errands a defined amount of time so that they don't eat the day up.

- Acknowledge that sometimes, staring at the computer screen isn't the best way to get the job done. Especially if you're at the computer for most of the work day, consider an "exercise desk" where you can work while on a treadmill or exercise bike, or make an hour of outdoor exercise part of your work day.

Also, I think that productive people are sometimes defined more by what they don't do rather than what they do. For example, our household doesn't have broadcast TV and we watch one or two movies per month on DVD. If you watch a couple of Netflix movies a week, you could probably start a blog, write a book or market your translation work to better-paying clients in the same amount of time you spend watching movies. However, our household also considers nightly home-cooked meals to be an essential component of our day. We spend a fair amount of time growing, shopping for and preparing food, but we feel it's an overall benefit to our quality of life. A big part of increasing your productivity is prioritizing the activities that are important to you and eliminating those that aren't. As the summer winds down, it's a good time to think about your goals for the upcoming months and how you can achieve them efficiently!

4.7 The second half

International Translation Day is coming up at the end of this month; this year's theme is Translation: Bridging Cultures (I like it!). Karmically enough, ITD is also my (and my husband's... is that karmic enough for you?) birthday, and this year it's a big one. Although I don't think I'm in mid-life crisis mode over turning 40, it has occurred to me that at least from a statistical point of view, I'm knocking on the door of the second half of life. And I do think that any big milestone is a good opportunity for reflection, so I'd like to solicit some input from readers who are past the halfway point themselves. Specifically, what changes have you made in your work life (or what changes would you like to make) now that you're in mid-life? What have you re-evaluated and what have you kept the same? Here are some thoughts that have popped into my head so far:

- As I get older, I love translation more and more. Being a better translator is more important to me all the time. However, I find that I also get less tolerant of job stress; clients who needed the project yesterday are less and less appealing and rush work is more and more stressful.

- Translating stuff that hangs around for a while and that people actually read is more important to me. I've always loved international development translation for this reason, and it's why one of my goals for this year is to take a literary translation course.

- I find myself thinking more about my future work life. In part, this is because I had my daughter at what's considered a relatively young age here in Boulder (30). As compared to some of my friends who are in their mid-40s and have preschoolers, I'll be 48 when my daughter graduates from high school. That opens up lots of possibilities; teaching translation, getting an in-house job, going back to school, and so on. Right now I can't say that I'm hankering for a radical departure from what I do now, but it's interesting to think about.

4.8 What types of incentives work best for you

Especially when you work on your own, incentives can be an important part of succeeding in business (and in life, for that matter!). It's important to figure out what kinds of incentives work for you, so that you can use them to advantage. For example, you might encounter some of the following types of incentives in your business (and, disclaimer, I'm not a social scientist, so I'm sort of making up names for these!):

- The appeal of getting something you want once you reach a goal. This kind of incentive could be intrinsic; for example the feeling of accomplishment and success that you have when you finish a big project. Or it could be extrinsic; for example you might create small rewards for yourself like taking the evening off if you finish work early or large rewards such as taking 50% of the money from a large project and spending it on a weekend away.

- The fear of losing something you already have if you don't reach a goal. I recently read an interview with "Four Hour Work Week" author Tim Ferriss about his new book "The Four Hour Body." Although I'm a bit skeptical about the book's claims (and as someone who loves to sleep, I'm not even trying the two hours of sleep a night plan!), I thought that Ferriss had an interesting point about "Puritanical" (as he calls them) incentives. For example, Ferriss ponders why more health clubs don't operate on a payback plan, where you pay a certain amount of money at the start of the month and then every time you work out, you get some money back. So if you don't work out at all, you lose $400 a month; but if you work out 16 times or more, your membership becomes free. In the business world, you could put this into action by taking a chunk of money and putting it into an escrow account (which could be a separate bank account or an envelope in your desk drawer). If you achieve a certain goal by the deadline you've set, you get to spend the money on whatever you want. But if you don't reach the goal, you have to scatter the money in a park near your house, donate it to charity, etc.

- Public humiliation or social pressure. Ferriss also talks about this type of incentive, and suggests that the money-back health club could take photos of its clients in their underwear, and if they don't work out often enough, post the photos on the health club website (!). I doubt that many people are dying to see photos of scantily clad translators, but public humiliation is a really good incentive. When I delayed and delayed in finishing the second edition of my book, I was so mortified by the number of people who kept asking about it (including in public forums) that the social pressure was a really good incentive to finish!

I think that the key here is figuring out what types of incentives or reward systems work well for you. For example I'm not very materialistic or very competitive, but I am very motivated to follow rules and to feel good about myself. When I've tried to come up with something to buy myself if I achieve a certain goal, I have a hard time even thinking of anything I want that much. But (and I admit that this sounds kind of juvenile!) when I did the Get Clients Now program, I found that just the thrill of completing all 10 of my daily marketing actions and checking them off on a goal sheet was a huge incentive. Also, I find that feeling a certain way (less stressed, more productive, etc.) is a big incentive for me, whereas getting a physical item is not so tempting. I've been able to use these observations to help design incentives that really mean something for me!

5 Client relations

5.1 What to send clients and colleagues for the holidays

When November rolls around, it's time to think about your end-of-year greetings/thank you plans for your clients and colleagues. Obviously these plans will vary depending on your country, customs, budget and time limits, but here are a few suggestions for spreading some cheer, gratitude and name recognition.

Holiday greeting basics:

- Send something. OK; I know this sounds pitifully basic... but I think that even if you only have time to pick up a box of cards and sign them, you should at least do that. I've heard a few clients comment (in a good-natured way!) that they notice who sends something at the end of the year and who doesn't; and you know which of those groups you want to be in!

- That being said, go for a card that is high-quality and has a fairly universal image and message. Unless your clients are members of a specific religion or cultural group, it's best to pick a holiday card with a semi-generic "season's greetings" message and an image that isn't associated with a specific holiday. In our industry I think that the "around the world" motif (i.e. a globe with a dove, flags of various countries, "peace" in multiple languages, you get the picture...) is a little overused but can work if you find the right card. I think that two good choices are charity-themed cards (such as those from Unicef) or locally-themed cards (this year I ordered Colorado mountain scene cards for my clients and colleagues).

- Avoid pre-printed mailing labels. Address your cards by hand; remove any trappings of mass-production from your holiday greeting efforts.

- Don't forget your colleagues, especially those who refer work to you. For many of us, these people are some of our most powerful marketing tools. See below for ideas on how to really single them out!

Holiday greetings, beyond the basics:

- Personalize. If you have time, write something specific about that client or colleague. How you really appreciate their friendliness and attention to detail; how flattered you were to be selected to translate their annual report; how their trust and referrals have really helped your business grow. If you're a business or agency, think about having all of your employees sign the cards; I always enjoy it when my agency clients do this.

- Send gifts to your top clients and your top-referring colleagues. These don't have to be extravagant. Something like special chocolates, tea, a wreath or better yet, products that are made in your local area! Personally I would go with something unique that you select and send rather than something ordered from an office gifts catalog.

- Specifically thank your "multipliers." Thanks to Grant Hamilton of Anglocom (www.anglocom.com) for teaching me this term! Especially if you work with direct clients, you probably have an advocate within the company who loves your work and encourages her/his superiors to use your services. Think about sending two cards or gifts: one to the company as a whole and one to your multiplier.

- Here's a wacky one: a holiday letter to your clients. Here in the US, it's common for people to send a letter with their holiday cards, telling about what happened over the course of the last year. These letters are sometimes maligned for their braggy, "don't you wish you were as happy as we are???" tone, but personally I enjoy reading them. Obviously you want to write a separate holiday letter for your clients; one that details your professional progress such as conferences, awards, large projects, publications, etc. and also thanks your clients for their trust and confidence in you over the past year. I don't know... this one came to me while I was jogging this morning. Any thoughts?

- And then there are in-person visits at which you can present your holiday gift, thank the client for their business and find out how their year went. I think this is a high-investment, high-value strategy. I know of one medium-sized agency that visits nearly every one of their local clients during the holidays. Huge time outlay? You bet! Huge returns? Probably; especially if the competition is sending a low-quality card with a pre-printed mailing label.

5.2 Making translation easy versus making translation cheap

When you're inquiring about a professional service, let's say taxes, computer help or marketing consulting, which is more attractive to you: a service provider who seems ultra-competent and gives the impression that the process will be easy for you, or a service provider who charges low rates and gives the impression that the process will be cheap? While few clients are completely price-insensitive, I think that it's important to always be looking for ways to make your clients' lives easier and avoid bogging them down in the complexity of what you do.

For example, let's say that you need a really good small business accountant. You know that accountants charge fairly high rates; upwards of $100 an hour and maybe as much as $200 an hour, so you have a ballpark figure in mind. You call CPA #1 and explain your situation. His/her response: "Well, switching accountants at this time of year is complicated. If only you had called me in January. I need your personal and business returns for the past three years, don't give me the originals, you'll have to copy them and drop them off. I'm only here 10-4 outside of tax season so you have to come during those hours" and so on. At that point, do you even care how little this person charges? Even if this accountant's rates were below what I expected to pay, I would be turned off. I hate accounting, I hire an accountant to make my life easier, and this person has already bogged me down with too many details and too many hoops through which I have to jump.

But how about this: you call CPA #2 and explain your situation. His/her response: "No problem at all, thanks for calling. If you're interested in switching to us, you'll just need to sign a release form and then I'll call your current accountant and ask them to fax us your past returns. Our hours are shorter outside of tax season but we do everything electronically with password-protected files so you can scan and submit your documents whenever you want. Also if you're interested we could review your previous returns for errors or missed deductions and there's no cost to you unless we find something." At that point, I would be willing to pay the high end of the rate range I was expecting, because this person conveys the impression that my life will be immeasurably easier and I will save time (and therefore be able to work more and earn more money) by using his/her services.

Think about applying these types of scenarios to your own business:

- When you receive an inquiry from a client, assume that the client wants you to solve their problem, not give them a deal.

- Don't get pedantic. Think: do you really care about the minute details of your service providers' jobs? Right. Stick to the information that your client really needs.

- Think of simple ways to streamline things for your clients. If you always translate their quarterly newsletter, can you contact them on a predetermined date to talk about the next issue? Can you set up a secure file transfer site so that your clients can access their translations whenever they want?

Can you send them a short survey to ask how you can better meet their needs?

- Try to frame things positively. Not "I can't finish it by Thursday morning unless you can get it to me by Wednesday noon," but "If you can get that to me by Wednesday noon, I could definitely have it back to you by the time you get into the office on Thursday."

- Don't make translation sound easy (we know: it's not!), make the client feel that you will make things easy for them.

5.3 Passing as "one of them": the client Turing test

During Speaking of Translation's recent interview with Chris Durban, Chris mentioned an excellent quality metric for specialized translators: the 10-minute Turing test. A Turing test involves a human attempting to determine if he/she is having a discussion with a computer or with another human. For example, many of you probably remember the ELIZA program, which simulated a psychiatric consultation and was often considered as having passed the Turing test. And as a complete aside, if you're interested in Alan Turing and his era, you really have to read Neal Stephenson's *Cryptonomicon*, often described as "the ultimate geek novel."

But back to Chris' advice. In order to pass the translation client Turing test, she advises that we translators should be able to pass as professionals in our field(s) of specialization for at least ten minutes. For example if you're a medical translator, you should be able to attend a medical conference and at the end of a ten-minute technical conversation with other attendees, you reveal that you're actually a translator and the attendees say "I can't believe you're not a doctor/nurse/medical instrument engineer/etc." For example, Chris does financial translation for some of France's leading corporations. During the webinar, she pointed out that this Turing test goal motivates her to stay on top of the world financial news (i.e. the Greek debt crisis), not just the specific topics about which she translates. This gives her greater credibility with her clients, differentiates her from kinda-sorta-specialized financial translators and greases the wheels of conversation when she meets her clients in person.

Fabulous advice: now let's look at how this works in practice. About six months ago, I decided that I wanted to deepen my own knowledge of international development, one of my primary areas of specialization. I'm not sure I'm at the "I thought you worked for the World Bank!" point yet, but I do feel like I'm improving. Here's an outline of what I did, and of course feel free to add your own experiences as well.

- Took some baby steps. I joined the Society for International Development which gets me a subscription to their excellent professional journal, information about their events, and the all-important membership card (wait, maybe I am already an expert!). I also signed up for e-mail newsletters from entities such as Devex, which got me somewhat tuned in to the international development buzz: who's hiring, who's working where, who's in the news all the time, that kind of thing.

- Plugged in to social media. I started following a bunch of international development entities on Twitter, and I also started reading some blogs that I pegged as the more widely-read international development blogs. These included Owen Abroad, NextBillion, Partners in Health, USAID Impact and Global Development: Views from the Center. As Chris commented, I found that these blogs were not exclusively, or even primarily, related to the work that I do. Some of these blogs don't relate at all to French-speaking countries that receive international development aid. But all of them relate to the sector as a whole, and that's really helped broaden my knowledge. I also feel much more informed about some of the "hot" issues in international development, such as pay-for-performance development funding, in which countries get aid based on the results that they achieve, not on the programs that they plan to implement.

- Got a teeny tiny bit involved. Over time, I mustered the courage to comment on some of these blogs. I'm not sure that anything earthshaking came of it, but I felt like for once, I had done some actual contributing and networking outside the translation industry.

- Forced myself to do extra research. I've been translating French international development documents long enough that I know the terminology pretty well. But on my recent projects, I've forced myself to go beyond terminology and do some real research. There's a big difference between knowing that *chaîne du froid* means "cold chain" and being able to explain what a cold chain is, why it's so hard to maintain one in a developing country, what happens when it malfunctions and how new technology like solar power is changing the appliances that can be used in the cold chain. I found this research both very time-consuming and very satisfying.

There's still room for improvement. I really need to attend some in-person events, but I just couldn't work my schedule around last week's Society for International Development World Congress. I also really need to have some one-on-one meetings with people who work in international development to find out how their translation procurement works (most of my current ID clients have come as referrals, or they found me rather than the other way around). But overall, I feel like this effort has really boosted my confidence and competence. Thanks to Chris for this great advice!

5.4 Getting the names straight

One of the great things about our industry is the variety of people we get to work with; people from all different countries, cultures and ethnic and linguistic backgrounds. The other side of this coin is that we have a lot of clients and colleagues who aren't named

Bob or Janet, which brings up a few issues that we need to pay attention to:

- Get the spelling right. Take this from someone who receives e-mail addressed to Corrine, Corrinne and even "Hey Connie!" (from someone I've never met). If someone has an uncommon name, copy their name from the e-mail that they sent you so that you get it right. When it comes to first impressions, there really is no bigger turnoff than being addressed by the wrong name.

- Call people what they ask to be called. In some cases, people want to be called by a name that isn't their given name, and really that's their prerogative. I learned this lesson when I kept insisting to an Asian acquaintance that I wanted to try using her Chinese name, rather than Veronica, the name she used in English. Finally she explained that it pained her to hear English speakers butcher her Chinese name, and she'd really (really) rather be called Veronica. Another Asian friend told me that he (emphasis on "he") asked to be called Scott rather than his Chinese name, Hoa, because he was "tired of getting rejection letters addressed to 'Dear Ms. Ly'." So, use the name that your client or colleague asks you to use.

- Use titles wisely. Similar to French's use of *tu* and *vous*, it's sometimes hard to know when to use a title and when to use someone's first name. In general if you're contacting a prospective client, a title is a safe bet. In English, always use "Ms." for women even if you know that the person is married. Again, take this from someone who receives e-mail to "Dear Mrs. McKay," which is actually my mother, since I don't use my husband's last name. The place where I think it's good to omit a title is when you want to put someone at ease; when someone is contacting you as the employer/authority/job reference, etc. and you want to let them know that you're really not that scary, I think it's good to respond to the "Dear Mr. Warren" e-mail with "Dear

Celeste, thanks for your message and feel free to call me Paul."

- Gender. This is a hard one. If you have a name that is used for both genders (Chris, Alex, Terry, etc.) or a name for which the gender is not obvious to English speakers, you may or may not want to clarify your gender. It's easy to do with a simple "Ms. Alex Thomas" or "Mr. Fouad El Tawil" in your e-mail signature file, but of course it's up to you whether or not you want to do this.

5.5 Dear Client...

Interestingly enough, I've been asked more than once, "How does a freelance translator fire a client?" Although "part ways with" might be a better term than "fire," this phenomenon definitely exists, and is a customer relations issue that translators have to deal with. I think that there are a few reasons for this: the supply and demand situation in our industry means that highly skilled translators may be interested in raising their rates and leaving their lower-paying clients behind; raising rates often means look-ing for new clients, and unfortunately there are translation clients out there who are very problematic to work with. To be fair, we'll agree that the same is true of freelancers, and that clients are also sometimes forced to sever the relationship with translators, but in this post we'll look at when and how to politely write a Dear Client letter.

To me, the primary rule of client interaction is "act with class." Regardless of the issue you need to address, remain professional; don't get personal, don't get nasty, don't sling mud. At the same time, I think that it's fine to tell the truth about your reasons for severing the client/translator relationship if you want to, and that it's also fine to say as little as possible, this is really a personal decision. Always keep in mind that the translation industry is a small one and is also very word-of-mouth driven; avoid burning bridges whenever possible. Let's look at a few scenarios and possible ways to communicate with your client.

Scenario: A new client contacts you with an offer of a project. You look them up on your favorite translation client rating list (you have one, right? and you always check it before working with a new client, right?) and find that they are a known non-payer or late payer.

Possible responses: 1) Very brief "no thank you" message, not addressing the issue 2) I'll admit that although I don't give specific information in this type of message, I do let the agency know why I'm declining the offer, for example "Translation industry ratings of your company are such that I must decline to work with you at this time unless you are able to pay in advance by wire transfer or credit card."

Scenario: You have raised your rates beyond what a long-time client will pay, but the client continues to contact you with offers of work at your old rates; let's assume that other than the rates, you enjoyed working with this client. For what it's worth, this is the scenario that I've been asked about more than any other.

Possible responses: I would address this politely but directly, for example: "Thank you for your message. While I do appreciate your ongoing offers of work and have enjoyed working with you in the past, I have, as you know, raised my base rate to X cents per word. Please feel free to contact me if you have any projects for which you have a budget of X cents per word and I will be happy to take a look at them."

Scenario: A client has become very problematic to work with. We'll assume that this client doesn't owe you money, but that you no longer want to work with them in any capacity.

Possible responses: 1) Brief and to the point: "Effective immediately, I no longer wish to be considered for assignments from your agency. Please remove me from your list of available freelancers." I wouldn't advise this unless you really, really don't want to ever hear from this client again, but it gets the point across effectively. 2) Addressing the issue in some way while remaining professional: "Due to some differences between your work style and mine, I have decided to focus my translation work on other clients. Please remove me from your list of available freelancers. Best regards, etc."

Scenario: A client that you otherwise enjoy working with cannot pay you more than what you are currently charging, and you have decided to raise your rates.

Possible responses: To me, this is the hardest type of situation to handle, especially if you have been working with the client for a long time. In this scenario, I would always leave the door open for working with the client in the future; emphasize that you are terminating the relationship at this time, but that you are open to renegotiating in the future. For example, "Although I have always enjoyed working with your agency and hope to do so in the future, I understand that my new base rate of X cents per word is outside the range of rates that you are able to pay at this time. If in the future you are able to consider higher rates, please let me know and I will be very interested in working with you again."

5.6 Using objective data to set your translation rates

Possibly the most anxiety-provoking aspect of launching or running your translation business is deciding how much to charge. Charge too much and you'll be priced out of the market; charge too little and you'll be working overtime just to make ends meet. The easiest way to remove the anxiety from this decision is to gather some objective data such as how much money you would like to make and how much it will cost you to run your business.

Adding to the pricing confusion is that most people are used to calculating their wages by the hour, rather than by the word. Beginning translators often don't know how to estimate how long a translation will take, so don't know how to set their per-word rates in order to reach their target hourly rate. Whereas an experienced linguist knows approximately how many words per hour he or she translates when working on various types of documents: general, technical, highly technical, handwritten, hard copy, HTML, etc., there is no way to know this if you haven't done much translation; you simply have to time yourself while you translate to see how fast you work.

In general, a translator who is a relatively fast typist (or uses speech recognition software that works well) can translate 400-600 words per hour or 2,000-3,000 words per day, but this is only a ballpark figure. When working on a highly technical document, even an experienced translator might work as slowly as 150 words an hour, and I once worked on a project where I consistently translated up to 1,000 words per hour because the document was non-technical and very repetitive.

First, complete the following calculation using your actual or estimated totals:

- Hours per week you would like to work

- Weeks per year you would like to work (subtracting vacation weeks)

- Multiply the above two items to get your total working hours per year

- If you foresee taking sick time or additional legal holidays off, subtract those hours

- Subtract your non-billable time, normally 25-50% of your total work time, for marketing, accounting, meetings, slow work periods, etc.

- This is your total billable hours per year

Now, calculate how much money you need/want to earn, by adding together:

- Your salary goal in dollars

- Taxes (15-50% of salary)

- Internet, web hosting, phone, fax, cell phone

- Professional memberships and continuing education

- Marketing materials and advertising

- Office supplies

- Computer hardware and software; technical support

- Auto and travel expenses

- Other costs of operation such as work-related child care, office rent, website development, etc.

- Add the above items together to get your total cost of business operation

- Then, divide your total cost of business operation by your billable hours from the first calculation, which will show your required hourly rate

Once you have this hourly rate worksheet completed, you've completed a major step in pricing your translation services. Your next step is to determine how you're going to arrive at that hourly rate. For example if you want to earn $60.00 an hour, you can achieve this by translating 600 words per hour at 10 cents per word, 400 words per hour at 15 cents per word or 300 words per hour at 20 cents per word. In order to do this, you need to know how fast you work (the only way to figure this out is to time yourself while you do some translations) and what the range of rates for your language pair(s) and specialization(s) is. For example, you might look at rates surveys on online translation marketplaces, the ATA compensation survey or look at websites of translators in your language pair to see if they publish their rates. Some translators, although not all, are also willing to discuss rates with their colleagues.

Knowing how much you need to charge also tells you what type of clients you need to look for. For example, if your hourly rate goal is high, you may need to market to direct clients rather than to translation agencies, or at least to very high-end translation agencies. In working with beginning translators, I find that work speed is often an issue for them and it impacts their work in a few ways. First, a translator whose work is solid but who translates 250 words an hour is going to struggle to make a living on typical agency rates. Second, agencies understandably like working with translators who can turn around large documents in a short amount of time, and won't be thrilled to hear that it will take you four days to finish 5,000 words.

Yet another element that enters into the rates equation these days is currency exchange rates. If you work in the US and bill in euros, for example, you may make 20% more in dollars if you bill the client in euros. This may affect your choice of where to look for clients and what currency to bill in, so it's important to consider exchange rates when you set your prices and when you decide how to be paid.

5.7 Dispute resolution in the translation industry

For better or for worse, the translation industry does not currently have a standard procedure or body for resolving disputes between translators and clients. So, clients who feel that a translator has delivered substandard work and translators who feel that they've been unfairly treated by clients do not have a standard avenue of recourse and must either resolve the issue themselves or pursue it through traditional legal means such as small claims court or collections services.

A typical translation industry dispute situation often goes like this:

Translator: "My translation was perfect and now the client is refusing to pay. Several of my friends even looked over the translation and agreed that it was perfect. The client has to pay me."

Client: "The translator came highly recommended but the translation is horrible, unusable. We've nearly lost one of our biggest clients because of this. We shouldn't have to pay for this work."

Disputes between translators and clients arise over various issues; quality issues are the stickiest, since they are so subjective. In other areas, a dispute may arise but it's more clear-cut: either the translator met the deadline or didn't; either the client paid on time or didn't. But when it comes to quality, it's often a "your word against mine" situation that quickly turns acrimonious. Following are some tips for avoiding and resolving dispute situations, both from the translator's point of view and the agency's.

First, every translator should belong to an a translation agency rating service such as Payment Practices or the ProZ Blue Board and should check it before accepting a job from any new client. To me, this is an absolute requirement of running a successful freelance business; recently, I received several e-mails from translators complaining about a non-paying agency. In about two minutes spent on Payment Practices, the agency rating service I subscribe to, I was able to see that this agency had a track record of non-payment going back several years. While these translators certainly didn't deserve not to be paid, I see no excuse for not investing $15 or $20 per year and a few minutes of your time to check out what other translators think of a potential client.

Second, translators need to be honest about their abilities; the vast majority of the quality issues I hear about (in which the translator admits that he/she did a poor job) involve a situation where the translator took the job for the wrong reasons: was afraid to say no, really needed the money, didn't look at the documents before accepting, etc. Finally, translators need to be able to hear and learn from feedback about their work. Here in freelance-land, we don't have annual performance reviews, and even those of us who are ATA-certified take the certification test only once, so outside assessments of our work are few and far between. If a client has legitimate complaints about your work, take them as a learning opportunity and avoid getting defensive; apologize and ask what you can do to regain the client's trust.

From the client perspective, vetting a translator ahead of a job is somewhat harder, since there aren't yet any services devoted to critiquing specific translators. A translator might be asked to provide references, but chances are that these will be positive. And, as with investments, "past results are not always an indicator of future performance." Even a qualified translator will have an off day, technical problems, etc. and either miss a deadline or deliver substandard work.

I think that when this happens, the most important thing from the client's perspective is to provide specific examples of what was wrong with the document, not just say "It was terrible and we're not paying you." For example, a client could provide a document with tracked changes, indicating the revisions that an editor made. Or, the client could provide a list of specific examples that show why the document had to be retranslated. If the document was sent to the end client without being reviewed and the quality objections are coming from the end client, the document should be reviewed by another translator before the quality objections are addressed, since the end client's objections may or may not be valid.

The hardest-to-resolve situation arises when all of the above steps have happened and there's still no agreement on whether the translation is acceptable or not. This brings up the question of whether a standard dispute resolution procedure or a dispute resolution organization is something that would benefit the translation industry overall. What we're missing right now is a neutral arbitration setting, where the translation can be evaluated by someone who has no stake in the outcome. As it stands, the translator is likely to call in a colleague who is in turn likely to agree with him or her that the translation is fine, while the agency is likely to use another translator it works with, who will probably agree that the translation isn't up to snuff. As of now, in the U.S. at least, there is no third party who will intervene in this type of dispute; maybe it's a niche waiting to be filled?

5.8 Vetting prospective clients and job offers

One of the most frequent questions that I see from beginning translators is how to decide if a new client or a job offer is legitimate. It's a delicate process, and it's not an exact science. Sometimes even experienced translators get scammed, and sometimes a client that seems a little shady during the first contact turns out to be quite trustworthy. Following are a few tips on this issue.

First, always (always!) use a translation industry client rating list to see if the prospective client has been rated there. I belong to and swear by Payment Practices (www.paymentpractices.net) and I check it immediately when a new agency client contacts me. In my experience, known non-payers have generally been rated on Payment Practices or a similar list, so these services are an invaluable resource.

I also think it's completely acceptable to ask a prospective client for references from other translators as long as you offer the same in return. Ask if the client is a member of a professional association for translators or translation companies. This is not an absolute guarantee of legitimacy, but it indicates that the client is at least willing to invest the time and money in joining such an association. In addition, never work for a client without getting full contact information including physical address, telephone number, and the name and contact information for the person who handles accounts payable.

Asking for advance payment is also an option, especially if you are not in dire need of the work that the client is offering. This type of arrangement might involve full advance payment, partial advance payment, or a partial advance payment and then another installment once you've submitted part of the translation. Some clients will agree to this type of payment plan and some will not, since the client then runs the risk that a translator who has already been paid either does not return the translation or returns an unacceptable translation. In my case, I ask all clients who are not established businesses to pay in advance, since (I learned this the hard way) it's actually not very hard for an individual to disappear after receiving the translation, for example by moving without a forwarding address or phone number.

Part of the vetting process is not quantifiable, but rather involves using your intuition about a client. I've found that just the process of politely asking a client about some of the issues above can go a long way toward avoiding a non-payment situation before it starts. When a less than solvent client knows that they've landed on a translator who checks industry rating lists, asks for references from current translators and clarifies the payment terms and methods up front, they're likely to seek another, less savvy translator.

5.9 When a client is dissatisfied

No matter how meticulous you are about a) your translations and b) your business practices, you can't work as a freelancer without dealing with disgruntled clients from time to time. First, let's say this: unless you love interpersonal conflict, dealing with unhappy clients is awful. Running your own business means caring very deeply about your work and putting your reputation behind every translation that you do, and it can be a truly horrible experience to have a client question your competence, integrity, whatever. But since this situation is bound to occur, let's look at what you can/should do after you receive that angry phone call or e-mail from a client.

For the purposes of this post, let's assume that the client's complaint has at least some basis in fact. Maybe you don't see the problem as being as serious as the client does, but you agree that there's some shred of an issue to be dealt with. Baseless client complaints are another issue altogether, and one that I'll save for another post (or better yet, another translation blogger can take that one on!). I think that resolving legitimate disputes boils down to three basic steps:

- Admit to the mistake;

- Apologize;

- Try to make it better.

Admittedly, I'm a pretty conflict-averse person, and I'm also very committed to maintaining a good reputation in the translation industry. Therefore, I probably go a little further with these steps than some translators do. For example, if I make a legitimate error, I nearly always offer the client some sort of compensation: I once e-mailed a client the wrong file for a (thankfully) very small project the night before I was leaving for a vacation. When I returned from vacation and realized what had happened, I told the client that of course I didn't expect to be paid for that project, but that I also wanted to do a small job for them for free in the future. I think that this type of gesture shows the client that I get it: that freelancing can be a "one strike and you're out" type of business, and that I am very committed to client satisfaction.

A few other dispute resolution tips that I've gleaned over the years:

- When you receive an angry e-mail from a client, first, do nothing. Don't respond when you are angry too. Wait until you've cooled off a bit, then compose your response. Or compose your response and let it sit for an hour, then read it over before you send it.

- Always ask for specific examples of quality issues. It's really hard to know how to make it better with a client who says "The tone isn't what we wanted," "The terminology wasn't right for our audience," etc. Always ask for an edited version of your translation, or for a few specific examples of the kind of issues the client is talking about.

- Resist the urge to write a lengthy explanation in response to a client complaint. When you respond, be concise, be kind and admit what happened. "I really apologize for neglecting to fully comply with your style sheet; I agree with the changes that you made to the document and I want to assure you that I will be more meticulous about this in the future" is enough. Save the venting and ranting for your trusted circle of friends and colleagues!

- Don't complain about the client's requirements after the fact. If the client sends you a 12 page style guide for a 1,500 word project, or expects you to go through an arduous QA process with no increase in your rate, the time to lodge your objection is before the project starts.

- Don't take it personally. Clearly, this is easy to say and very, very hard to do. But when you're dealing with a business issue, try to keep it businesslike. Stay calm, stay polite and try to see things from the client's point of view.

- After the complaint is resolved, decide whether this client is a good fit for you. Sometimes the client's complaint reflects the fact that their work style and yours are not a good fit. And really, that's OK. There is enough other work out there for you, and there are enough other translators out there for them.

6 Translation technology and home office setup

6.1 Options for home office phone service

Lately I've been thinking about phone service for the home office. I've had a custom ring number (an extra phone number that runs over my home phone line but rings differently) ever since I started freelancing. At the time, Internet telephony was not a well-developed option and I didn't want to switch exclusively to a cell phone for work. Here's a look at the various home office phone options I've found, along with a few pros and cons for each.

- A plain old land line is the most straightforward option. If you live alone or don't have small children, you can probably get away with one line for work and personal use. However, if you need to have a second land line installed, the process can be expensive especially if you have to have additional phone jacks put in.

- The aforementioned custom ring number is great in that it's inexpensive ($5 per month through our local phone company), doesn't require an additional physical phone line and gives you a way to distinguish between business and personal calls. But there are a few downsides, which are becoming more of an issue for me now that I work for more direct clients. The custom ring number and the main number have to share an outgoing voice mail message, so either my clients get to listen to the "you've reached the home of... and the home office of... " message, or I have to put an office-only message on the home line. Also, only the main number is displayed on the caller ID when I phone someone, so my clients have occasionally redialed that number. Then when I answer, I think it's a personal call when it's actually a work call (awkward if one happens to be cooking dinner with a group of friends when a client calls!). In addition, it is not possible to forward the custom ring number to another phone without forwarding the main number at the same time.

- A business cell phone is another option, and not a bad option if you need or want a smartphone for work. Keeping the cell phone for business use should allow you to tax-deduct the bill, and you don't have to worry about how to handle your phone calls when you're out of the office. Two issues keep me from switching to a business cell phone: I would need one with an international calling plan (expensive) and as much as I try to be adaptable, I just hate talking on cell phones for long periods of time. I do have a cell phone that I use to check my work messages when I'm not home, but I wouldn't want to use it as my exclusive work phone.

- Because of these issues (largely the separation of voice mail and forwardability), I'm thinking of switching to Internet phone service. Due to issues with emergency calling, I wouldn't switch my main phone to an Internet-based system, but it's not an issue for my work phone. In addition, most of the main Internet phone services do enable call forwarding, so if I want to answer work calls when I'm not in the office, I can forward the work line to my cell phone. I've been looking at a few plans such as Vonage Lite, some of which are around $10 per month.

6.2 Why you need good web hosting: a cautionary tale

Ever since I launched my new professional website about a month ago, I've been meaning to remove my old website from my hosting account (can you tell where this is headed?). On Monday morning I had a bit of unscheduled time so I decided to take care of this. I'm fairly compulsive about doing technical tasks the right way, so I logged in to my web hosting account via FTP, then called my sysadmin husband to verify that I was doing the right thing, then called my ISP's tech support to verify that I was doing the right thing. Here's where the problem started: I explained my plan to the tech support rep as "I just navigate into the correct folder and then delete all of the files for the old site, right?" To which he correctly responded "Yes!" and offered to walk me through the deletion process. I declined (bad idea 1.0) because I was sure I knew what I was doing and didn't want to waste his time.

After I got off the phone, I thought I had an even better plan: instead of deleting my old site page by page, I would just delete the whole folder that it was in (bad idea 2.0). So I highlighted the "WWW" folder in my account, clicked delete, clicked the "are you really sure" box and happily watched as the file names for all the deleted pages in my old site scrolled by; fantastic! A moment later, my delight turned to abject horror as file names for my new site popped up in the "deleted files" box. It took me a minute to realize what was happening, and then another minute to find the "stop" button on the FTP tool, but in that amount of time I had blown away enough pages that my new site was gone from the web. Worse, I had just sent out a bunch of links to a new article I'd written for translation clients. And I hadn't backed up the new site since it went live. And my web designer's programmer was on vacation and unreachable. I'm a pretty low-key person, but I literally screamed alone in my office when I realized what I'd done.

Here's where things started to get better: in ten years of being married to my IT support, I've learned something. When you really mess up a tech task, your first priority is to not make it worse. So instead of following my panic-driven impulse to just click stuff and try to fix what I'd done, I went out to the kitchen and drank a glass of passion fruit juice. This calmed me down enough that I decided to call my web hosting provider and just admit what I'd done. Hi, it's me, the one who didn't need you to walk me through the process of deleting the old site... well, guess what I managed to do?

And here's why it's worth paying $20 a month for web hosting from a really high-quality ISP. The first thing that Front Range Internet's tech support told me was "No problem, we'll just re-store your site from last night's backup." This took, no kidding, about 3 minutes. Then, they looked in their FTP log to figure out what I did to blow away the new site (hint: NEVER delete entire folders from your web hosting account unless you really know what you're doing. Just delete the individual files in the folders). Better still, the people at FRII were totally pleasant, didn't make me feel like an idiot (which they would have been completely justified in doing) and made the whole thing seem like no big deal. Morals of this story:

- If you have a website for your freelance business, back it up right this second.

- Then, call your web hosting provider and ask how often they run backups and how long it would take to restore your site if you did something terrible to it.

- If the answer to that question isn't satisfactory (i.e. your hosting provider doesn't back your site up), switch hosting providers ASAP.

6.3 Staying comfortable in the home office

One of the appealing aspects of working from home is that you're free to configure your work environment however you want, especially if you have a dedicated office room in your house. I recently gave my office a thorough cleaning and used the occasion to evaluate the ergonomics of my setup. Here are what I think of as some critical elements of feeling good and being productive at home:

- Good light is absolutely essential. I love this about my office: my desk is centered between two north-facing windows and two west-facing windows, so I have lots of natural light without a lot of glare. I use an overhead light but I find that a desk lamp creates too much direct light for my taste.

- I'm addicted to two large monitors. This used to require a second video card in your computer, but most late-model computers will now support two monitors without a lot of reconfiguring. With two 21-inch (or larger) monitors, you can have a pretty good view of four documents at once: for example I often translate with the French and English documents side-by-side on one monitor and an online dictionary and the project glossary side-by-side on the other. The only downside is that I've lost the ability to translate using only one monitor!

- For your hands' sake, invest in a keyboard that you really like. It seems like a small thing, but if your hands are going to be striking this thing 40 hours a week, you want the experience to be pleasant. I cannot speak highly enough of Unicomp keyboards; they are the descendant of the legendary IBM "buckling spring" keyboard which gives you a very audible "click" when you strike the keys. I have the SpaceSaver 104 model ($79) and I love it so much that I clean it with rubbing alcohol on Monday mornings to keep it grime-free (seriously; just don't tell too many people!).

- What you sit on has a lot to do with your in-office comfort too. I'm not a huge fan of the traditional office chair because I often end up sitting sideways with my legs crossed which is obviously not great from the circulation or posture point of view. I've thought about trying a kneeling chair, but my favorite office chair is actually a $20 fitness ball that I've had for years. I like fitness balls because it's physically impossible to sit on one with your legs crossed, and they encourage you to sit in a neutral (non-hunched) position.

- I'm not a neat freak, but I do think that a relatively clutter-free office is key to productivity. I find that if there are piles of stuff around me, I think about cleaning them up rather than what I should be working on. I also like to keep some of my favorite family pictures and pictures of my favorite vacation places where I can see them from my desk.

- Sound is a big contributor to workplace comfort as well. I listen to music only if I'm doing something totally mindless like entering receipts into my accounting program. Once in a while if I'm working very late at night, I'll listed to disco music on my iPod just to stay awake. At the same time, I don't like a totally quiet environment when I'm working during the day. I'll admit this is a weird behavior, but my preferred sound environment is to leave the radio in the kitchen on NPR (news/talk radio) so that I can hear the sound of voices but I can't make out what they're saying. For some reason this is just enough background noise for me to focus and not enough noise that it's distracting.

6.4 Why netbooks are better than smartphones

Back in the summer of 2009, I wrote about my decision to purchase a netbook. Over a year later, my Asus Eee is still going strong and I still love it. I paid around $300 via Newegg.com and I haven't had any software or hardware problems with my netbook despite some heavy use. And it's really, really small and light.

At the time I wrote my 2009 post, I was hemming and hawing between a netbook and a smartphone. I understand many of the reasons that people use and love smartphones, but I've since come to believe that at least for my purposes, a netbook is a much better option. Because:

- It forces you to decide when you really need to work on the go. I'm firmly against being always on duty; I work hard while I'm working, and then I shut the computer off and go play. In fact, I think that there's growing evidence to suggest that people who work in the low to mid 30 hours per week are the most productive. If I owned a smartphone, I know that I would take it with me most of the time: why not use those few minutes while I'm waiting for my daughter at school or standing in line at the supermarket? But, at the risk of sounding like a Luddite, where do those "few minutes" end, and why not engage with the offline world for a few minutes? With a netbook, I only take it with me when I really need it, but because it's so small, I do take it sometimes. My family recently went on a multi-day bike trip while I was working on a book translation. I was faced with the option to work three or four 12-hour days before we left, or to take the netbook with me and work at night on the trip. I chose the latter, stuck the Eee in my bike bag (no kidding, it fits in a bike panier!) and felt much less stressed. My Eee also fits in the messenger bag that I use as a purse, so I take it when I get my car's oil changed or when I know I'll be stuck waiting somewhere for a long period of time.

- You can do real work on it. My typing accuracy on my Eee is only marginally lower than on my desktop's keyboard. By contrast, I think that a lot of e-mails that people write from smartphones have a smartphone quality to them; that's OK if it's a quick note to a colleague, but I wouldn't want to respond to a client that way. And if I'm just reading the e-mails for the sake of reading them, why not just wait until I'm in my office? In addition, I think it can be really hard if not impossible to look at attached documents on a smartphone. My netbook has a 10 inch screen which is too small for some tasks (i.e. having multiple documents on the screen at once) but works well for word processing, reading PDFs and browsing the web.

- A netbook can do most of what a laptop can do. Full-size

laptops certainly aren't obsolete; if you need a big screen or a really big hard drive or a lot of processor power, a full-size laptop is probably still your best choice. Netbooks are pretty amazing for their size, but I don't think that running your speech recognition software on top of your translation memory program on top of your office suite would work very well on one. However, my netbook has completely replaced my full-size laptop for traveling (it has a standard VGA port so can be hooked up to a projector) and I wrote most of the second edition of *How to Succeed as a Freelance Translator* on it using a free DTP program called LyX.

Obviously the title of this article is an overstatement; if you work on projects for which you just need to monitor e-mails, I think that a smartphone can be a great choice. And I think that the urge to work too much pulls at all of us freelancers regardless of whether we have a smartphone or not. But I do think that netbooks are worth a look if you're in needs analysis mode!

6.5 Home or away?

In the past few months, I've spoken with a few translators who fall into a small but interesting group; people who hate working from home. One, who I'll be profiling in an upcoming post, switched to an in-house job after a lengthy tenure as a freelancer and says he's "never going back;" a couple of others are happy as freelancers but work at rented offices rather than from home.

Talking to these people made me realize that rather than endlessly touting the benefits of working from home, it's worth taking a look at the pluses and minuses of the home work environment. When I talked to the former freelancer who has gone in-house, he didn't seem torn about his decision in the least. His reasoning? He leaves the job at the office, gets paid vacation and training, doesn't worry about cash flow and, since he's paid by the hour, can take the time to do the job right rather than rushing to meet a deadline or keep the money coming in. The freelancers who work in rented offices mostly focused on one factor in their decision:

social isolation.

To me, the important element of this story is that it's worth exploring your options as a translator even if you don't think that working from home is for you. Personally, I could write a mountain of posts on the things I love about working from home: obviously, freedom and flexibility are at the head of the list. Also, I've learned from working at home that I work best in shorter, more focused periods of time; my work day is usually divided into a few chunks of two to four hours and I find that my mental energy gets diluted when I have to work a semi-continuous stretch of eight or nine hours. Also, I think that the logistical circumstances of each translator's life have a lot to do with that person's level of satisfaction with working from home. In my case, I feel that the home-based cards are stacked very much in my favor; my husband and many of my friends are either freelancers or work very flexible part-time schedules, I live in a semi-urban walkable neighborhood where the social stimulation of a café, the library or an exercise class is at most a few minutes away. Other people may dislike working from home because they find themselves in the opposite situation, living alone or with a spouse who is at work 12 hours a day, in a rural area or a suburb with little possibility of social interaction during the day.

The one aspect of home-based work that I'm still struggling with is one that I think is common to many home-based workers: fighting the urge to work whenever I'm at home. So, I've developed (and am still in the process of developing) strategies to combat this tendency: turning my work computer off and not answering my work phone when I'm not working, planning at least one activity out of the house every day, and setting a hard and fast "quitting time" that can only be broken if I have a deadline for the next morning.

6.6 Why I use free and open source software

Since I launched my freelance business in 2002, I have used free and open source software almost exclusively. This model has worked very well for me, and I think that it's enabled me to work better, faster and more affordably than if I had used the proprietary software equivalents. There are some not so lofty reasons for this: first, cheap is my favorite price, and free is even better, so the tightwad in me really, really likes the idea of low-cost and reliable computing. Second, when I married my tech support (a Unix administrator and free software evangelist) I vowed to love, honor and cherish my husband and forsake the products of a certain software company in the Pacific Northwest if I wanted to continue to get free 24x7 in-house computer help.

For freelance translators, free and open source software works really well for some tasks and fails dismally at others. I find OpenOffice to be a far more pleasant word processor than its proprietary equivalents, but no amount of work will make translation environment tools that run from within Microsoft Word (i.e.Wordfast Classic) work in OpenOffice. The incompatibility of Word macros and OpenOffice macros is just too great. However, in nearly a decade of freelancing, I've never had a client notice than any of my regular "Word" documents were created and/or edited in OpenOffice.org, thanks to OpenOffice's "Save as..." capabilities. So, it's a matter of checking out the tools that your particular freelance business requires. I've been very happy with:

- Ubuntu Linux (www.ubuntu.com): Linux distributions are the source of many a "chunky versus creamy peanut butter" debate, but in my office we've been quite happy with the release cycle and ease of installation of Ubuntu.

- Open Office (www.openoffice.org). This is probably my most-used piece of free software. It runs on Linux, Mac and Windows (that's alphabetical, BTW) and is extremely, extremely compatible with the market leader word processors, including if you need to create and/or edit documents in Microsoft Word format. The suite includes a word processor, spreadsheet, presentation program, database and drawing program.

- OmegaT translation memory software (www.omegat.org). OmegaT is a community-developed free and open source translation environment tool. The online user community is very active, and it's developed by translators, for translators.

- KMail e-mail client. Here is what I love about this e-mail program: when you type an e-mail that contains a word similar to "attachment," i.e. "attached," "attaching," "attachment," but you don't attach a file, KMail pops up a polite little dialog box that says "The message you have composed seems to refer to an attachment, but you have not attached anything. Do you want to attach a file to your message?" I can't count the dozens of times this feature has saved me from the "Sorry, here's the attachment" doubletake that I often receive from other people.

- In the spirit of disclosure, I do also keep Microsoft Office on my computer for word count purposes, and since I don't have a Windows computer, I run it using Crossover Linux. I've been considering testing a dedicated word count tool on Linux, but in the absence of that, I still use Word's word count so that my statistics match my clients' as closely as possible.

6.7 Translation memory discounts: yes, no, maybe?

The issue of translation memory discounts, whereby a translator charges a lower rate for words that appear as repetitions or fuzzy matches in a translation environment/CAT/TM tool, is a contentious one. On the one hand, a client might reasonably argue that changing "press the green button" to "press the red button" doesn't involve translating four words, but rather one word. On the other hand, a translator might reasonably argue that reading that sentence, finding the difference and changing it takes about as much time or maybe even longer than just typing the translation from scratch.

Translators and clients have a few options to choose from: no TM discount at all; a TM discount only for high level matches such as 100% matches and repetitions; or a graduated pricing structure where fuzzy matches down to a certain percentage, say 75% or even 50%, are priced at a certain percentage of the translator's per word rate.

At a past ATA conference, I heard a translator argue that there are two translation markets out there: the TM market and the non-TM market, and you have to decide which one you're going to compete in. While I'm not sure that the choice is as binary as that, I think there's some truth to the idea. Many legal and financial translators I know are rarely if ever asked to give discounts for repetitions, and use a TM tool mostly for their own consistency and productivity. On the other hand, many technical translators I know would be out of business if they didn't use TM and give discounts for repetitions.

For some projects, such as product manuals that are regularly updated, it seems to me to border on ridiculous not to give TM discounts since the majority of the text will be recycled. However, I understand translators' frustrations with clients who nickel and dime over every repeated word simply out of a desire to pay as little as possible for the translation.

7 Marketing and networking

7.1 LinkedIn strategies

I've received several questions from readers about connecting with people on LinkedIn (www.linkedin.com). Most of the questions are something like this: "I receive connection requests from people I don't know at all, with no explanation of who they are or how I might know them. Is it rude/unwise to just ignore these?" This brings up the issue of one's personal LinkedIn strategy, so I think it's worth exploring.

I don't invest an enormous amount of time on LinkedIn, but I do think that for purposes of findability, every freelancer should have a profile on LinkedIn or a similar site. These sites rank very highly on search engines, so if clients are scouring the Internet for a translator, there's a good chance that they will come across your LinkedIn profile. In addition, I use LinkedIn as a virtual business card file; it saves me from keeping track of the e-mail addresses of all of my business contacts. I also belong to several LinkedIn groups; I lurk more than I participate, but I still find them valuable.

People seem to have a variety of feelings about LinkedIn connections, ranging from:

- only wanting to connect with people who they know personally and work with, resulting in a potentially small but very high-quality network

- being willing to connect with new people, if those people provide an explanation of why they want to connect

- actively connecting with anyone, also known as the LION (LinkedIn Open Networker) strategy

I can see rationales for all of these strategies, but in general I think I take the second option most often. One reason I'm an active social media user is that my local client base is very small. Colorado is not as international business-oriented as the coastal states in the U.S., and the major industries here (mining, agriculture, renewable energy) are not areas in which I translate. So, I have to broaden my horizons if I want to keep finding new clients. For that reason, I've done some active cold-contacting on LinkedIn, mostly in the form of sending contact requests to people who are in some of the same LinkedIn Groups I'm in (with a free account, you cannot cold-contact just anyone on LinkedIn). I've explained that I'm a US-based French to English translator specializing in law, international development and non-fiction books and that I'm interested in expanding my contacts in that person's country/industry. In general I've found people to be very receptive to these types of contacts. At the same time, I am reluctant to accept contact requests from people whose names I don't recognize, and who provide no explanation beyond the pro forma "I'd like to add you to my professional network on LinkedIn" message.

7.2 Some thoughts on professional photographs

A big thank you to Chris Durban (www.prosperoustranslator. com)for suggesting this post topic!

Let's say that you want to hire a professional services provider: maybe a business accountant, a copyright attorney, a web designer or a marketing consultant. You're clicking through that person's website, and on their About page, you see a photograph. Great! It's always helpful to get a visual image of the person you're thinking of working with. But then you notice that the person's photograph is clearly from 20+ years ago, or was obviously taken in a drugstore photo booth, or features them and their pet ferret, or you can't really tell what the person looks like because they're facing away from the camera and their hair is in their eyes. Problem? Maybe! Let's ponder the issue of professional photographs for a second.

I had never used a professionally-taken photograph until about a year ago. My previous head shot photos were decent (hair brushed, facing the camera, no ferrets) but clearly not taken by a professional. I told myself that a) it doesn't really matter, I'm just a freelancer; b) a professional photo session is outside my budget and c) how different will the photo look anyway? Then, Judy Jenner (www.twintranslations.com) gave our local translators' association the idea of hiring a professional photographer to do head shots of a bunch of our members during one session. Eve Bodeux organized this and it was a huge success. Our photographer did head shots of 12 people in two hours at a cost of $40 per person, and we were really pleased with the results. Since then I've been using the picture I had taken during that session, and I do think that it's an asset to my marketing materials. So, why should you consider a professional photograph?

- It shows that you're willing to invest in your business. I am very frugal. I don't own a clothes dryer and I wash Ziploc bags. But when someone hands me a business card with "Get your free business cards at..." printed on the back, my immediate reaction is that this person is not even willing to invest $25 in their business in order to get real cards. Ditto with the professional photograph: it shows that you care.

- It conveys an impression of you as a person. Let's face it: working with a freelancer is a very personal relationship. And if people don't have a positive impression of you, they are less likely to work with you. A professional photograph can help establish you as approachable, personable, likable and other qualities that are desirable in a business associate.

- It's what other people do. I hate to play the "everyone else is doing it" card, but there's some truth to this. If you consider yourself on par with other consultant-type service providers, your marketing materials need to be at that level.

When you're having your photo taken, it's also worth thinking about the image that you want to convey to your potential clients.

For example at our local photo session, at least one member was concerned that she looks too young (clients think she is inexperienced/don't take her seriously) and at least one was concerned that she looks too old (clients think she is outdated). Our photographer had some good suggestions on how to stage and pose the photograph in order to counter those impressions. In addition, I think that professional photographers really are better at putting you at ease during the photo session. I dislike having my picture taken and I don't think I've very photogenic, but I was very happy with the photos that I got from this session.

7.3 Tips for promoting your freelance services

Michelle Vranizan Rafter's blog, WordCount, has an excellent post (www.michellerafter.wordpress.com/2008/04/28/10-ways-to-promote-your-freelance-writing) about ways to promote your freelance writing, most of which are applicable to translation as well.

When it comes to things like blogs, e-newsletters, podcasts and even websites, part of the appeal for translators is that the market is quite open. While some demographic groups (moms, artists and political junkies, to name a few!) seem eager to write and podcast as much as, or maybe even more than people want to read, translators are amazingly reticent about putting their thoughts out there. So, it's comparatively easy to draw a lot of readership or listenership to what you're doing.

Of the tips that Michelle offers, I also strongly agree with her advice to attend conferences and visit clients in person. As largely web-based workers, I think it's tempting for translators to think that e-mail does it all, without the need to even get out of your pajamas. In my own experience, every face to face encounter I've had with an existing or potential translation client has more than paid for itself.

Lastly, Michelle's advice about "being the best at what you do" is fantastic. Bottom line, being a compulsive overachiever is very good for business when you're self-employed. Take a look at Michelle's post for more excellent tips on marketing!

7.4 Translation-targeted resumés: pitfalls and best practices

What with the U.S. economy on a downward slide and the euro continuing its climb above U.S. $1.50, many translators are marketing these days. Following are some tips on writing a translation-targeted resumé that will pass muster with potential clients.

Let's start with the obvious but often overlooked: prominently state your language pair(s). It sounds crazy, but I've read many a translator's resumé that buried this most basic information deep within the body of the document. My advice: put your language pair(s) right below your name at the head of the resumé, like "Melissa Thomas, Italian to English Translator." I would avoid using the generic "Italian Translator;" if you are truly qualified to translate in both directions, put "Italian <> English Translator" or something equivalent.

Include some sort of geographical information, at least your city. Although I don't have a P.O. box myself, I think that a P.O. box is a good option for your work address since it avoids having to give out your home address.

Use a professional e-mail address. This is one of my top five pet peeves when it comes to translator resumés. Anything @hotmail.com or an address such as "beachbabe2008," "kittykat" or "soccergod" (and I'm barely exaggerating here!) doesn't belong on a professional resumé and is also likely to be caught by a client's spam filter. My advice: if you want a free e-mail address or prefer webmail, use Gmail, I think it's the most "legitimate" of the freebies. I think that the best e-mail address is one that's associated with a domain name that you own, so that you never have to change it if you change ISPs.

Double and triple-check your contact information. Make sure it's a) correct and b) information that is "durable;" don't include a cell phone number that you might be getting rid of.

Give specific examples of your translation work without violating client confidentiality. "Extensive experience in patent translation" is much less impressive than "Translated 100+ patents: topics include automotive components, household appliance components and packaging."

If you've been translating for a substantial amount of time (I would say three to five years, others might go longer or shorter), eliminate all non-translation work experience that isn't relevant to what you do. If you worked as an engineer and now translate engineering documents, it's worth leaving that information in. But if you switched careers completely, say from managing a restaurant to doing translation, I wouldn't include it.

Include something about your computer setup. If nothing else, this tells the client that you are reasonably technology-savvy. You can also inspire confidence by including "with daily backups," "dedicated backup computer," etc. If you use translation environment/CAT tools, you can also include them here, or not, depending on whether you want clients to know that you have them.

I'll admit to being a traditionalist when it comes to resumés, and I find fancy graphics, catchy slogans and "creative" formatting to be a turn-off. Also, I think that a photograph, which is common to include on a European-format resumé, is inappropriate on a U.S. one.

Some features I've seen and liked on other people's resumés: the date when the resumé was updated (makes it clear that the document is up to date); information about recent professional development such as conferences and courses; a few very brief testimonials from past clients.

Remember that you are applying for *language work*. Although poor grammar, typos and incorrect punctuation have become commonplace in business documents, be the exception. Show your potential clients that you are worthy of their language work by making your own work error-free.

Lastly, keep it brief. For use in the U.S., one page is best, two pages is an absolute maximum. Put the most important information first. Remember when your high school guidance counselor broke the news that after you had sweated and cried over your college applications for six months, the average admissions counselor would spend three minutes reading them? Have the same attitude toward your resumé and you're on the right track!

7.5 Moving on up

Sooner or later, a hardworking and capable translator in an in-demand language pair is ready to take the business to the next level. Let's say you're someone who has been in the industry for 5+ years, you consistently have enough or more than enough work and you'd like to transition from working for Your Average Agency (we'll call them YAA) to working for High-Quality Clients (we'll call them HQCs) who may be agencies or direct clients. Despite the generally gloomy economic mood in the U.S., recent information from sources such as Common Sense Advisory shows that the translation industry isn't feeling the recession pinch as of yet, so now is a good time to move on up! How are you going to do it?

Take a course in one of your areas of specialization. The majority of YAA's translators are probably self-taught in their specialization areas; you'll stand out when you contact HQCs and let them know that you recently took a course in medical terminology, contract law, php programming or stock trading. Look at your local community college, or online/correspondence offerings by Coursera or a similar outlet.

Go see the stuff you translate about in action. Make some phone calls and see if you can spend a few hours with a patent agent, at a pharmaceutical manufacturing facility or a coffee roasting plant. Go look at how that gizmo you translated the manual for actually works. Sit in court for a day or watch a local legislative body in session.

Write an article and send a copy to the HQCs you'd like to work for. Most of YAA's translators are too busy working at moderate rates to do this. Write for a translation industry publication such as the ATA Chronicle or your local translators association's newsletter, or better yet, for a trade publication that your prospective HQCs might be reading. Give them a little introduction to how the translation process works, how to find a high-quality translation provider and some pitfalls and best practices for having their materials translated.

Proofread on paper. I've done editing work for some YAAs, and I would estimate (and other translators I've talked to have agreed with this) that probably 70% of YAA's translators aren't proofing their work at all. Evidence: the "finished" document arrives with errors that have already been marked by the spell-checker. Maybe 20% of translators are proofing, but doing so on the screen. Evidence: errors that the spell-checker didn't catch, but an "on paper" reader would have. Then there's the final 10%, who do the full three-step process of doing the translation, proofing the draft on paper, inputting the changes and then reading the finished target document. Be one of those 10% and HQCs will be impressed.

Become a better writer in your target language. I think that English-language writing and editing courses are some of the best money I've ever spent on professional development, and good writing skills are something that sets HQC translators apart from YAA translators.

Give excellent customer service. When an HCQ calls, be pleasant and easy to work with. Bail them out of a bind, iron out their nightmare documents, fix what the cheap translator broke and...charge what your time is worth! To me, this is one of the key points of working for HQCs; you go the extra mile for them, because when you ask yourself, "Am I really getting paid enough to deal with this?" the answer is "Yes!"

8 Money matters

8.1 How much do freelancers earn? Is it enough?

Beginning freelance translators often want to know (understandably) how much they can expect to earn in our industry. Experienced freelance translators often want to know (understandably) whether they are earning enough for the effort they put into their businesses. So, what do freelance translators earn?

- The American Translators Association does a compensation survey every few years: you can purchase the entire report on their website or read the executive summary for free. The dates are a little confusing: the data tables in the summary say that they are from 2006, the file itself is named 2007 and the executive summary appeared in the ATA Chronicle in February 2008. According to this survey, the average full-time freelancer makes a little over $60,000; but US-based respondents reported a large income disparity according to whether or not they are ATA-certified (average income of $72,000 for certified translators and $53,000 for non-certified).

- The US Bureau of Labor Statistics has some information too, and it's even more disparate. The BLS reports that in May 2008, the average salary for translators and interpreters was about $38,000 (yikes), with the highest 10 percent earning over $69,000 and the average federal government language specialist earning an average of $79,000.

- PayScale.com has some snapshot info about translators and

interpreters, and it's also broken down by years of experience.

I think that the issue with most of these surveys is that they are not
specific enough to individual situations. For example, is someone
who works 35 hours a week and takes 6 weeks of vacation full
time or part time? Is someone who works at a client's office 2
days a week and works for freelance clients 3 days a week self-
employed or in-house? Should translation volume be taken into
account? If you earned $130,000 last year but you worked 70
hours a week with no vacation, should your income be pro rated
to a 40 hour work week with 4 weeks off? You get the picture!

Anecdotally, I think that most of the above-referenced surveys
are slanted toward the low end of the market. Back in 2008, I
wrote a blog post on Secrets of Six-Figure Translators, and since
then I've talked to many more freelancers who've either stated
or hinted that they earn over $100,000 a year. I think that if
you're very good at what you do and you market yourself fairly
assertively, there is enough work out there to earn at least $75,000
a year as a freelance translator even if you work with a mix of
agencies and direct clients. I'd say that at this point, all of the
translators I know who work exclusively with direct clients earn
at least $100,000 a year.

But the real question when it comes to income is: is it enough?
The "is it enough" question involves a lot of subjective factors,
because it ties into the subsidiary question of whether you'd be doing better if you had a different job. Here's where the subjectivity
comes in. For example in my case:

- I'm reasonably happy with my income as compared to how
  much I work. I earn more than the ATA average and my
  sense is that I work less (maybe even a lot less) than most
  freelancers do, partly because of my family and non-work
  commitments and partly because I think I'm more productive at 30ish hours per week. However when I look at how
  the benefits of my husband's in-house job (company-funded
  retirement plan, insurance, paid vacation, and so on) add
  up, it's a reality check. If I deduct 15.3% self-employment

tax (which I only pay on about half my income since I have an S-Corp), 4-6 weeks unpaid vacation and my self-funded retirement plan from what I make, the bottom line is decidedly different.

- But, then there are the subjective factors. I love where we live, and there are very, very few in-house jobs in our area for what I do. The only reasonable option, working for a government agency, would involve driving over an hour each way and a relatively inflexible schedule. It's very important to me to have a work schedule that meshes with my daughter's school schedule at least until she is old enough to be home alone. Realistically, if I wanted an in-house job that was close to my house and that would offer a similar level of flexibility to freelancing, I would probably be looking at earning less than half what I make now.

"Enough" also depends on where and how you live. $75,000 sounds like a decent chunk of money, but if you are not incorporated and thus pay self-employment tax on that entire amount, live in a nice apartment in a major city, have a car loan or student loan or credit card payment and fund your own health insurance and retirement, that amount goes pretty quickly. On the other hand if you live in a fairly rural area, are debt-free or close to it and practice freelance frugality, you could probably be saving 50% of your after-tax income if you gross $75,000 or more.

8.2 Putting 40 cents a word in context

Well, it seems that something about money and income always hits people's urge to discuss! At 65 comments and counting, "How much do freelance translators earn? Is it enough?" is far and away the most-discussed post in three years of Thoughts on Translation and everyone's comments have provided me with lots of food for more posts. Here's one: that elusive 40+ cents per word, which I would consider the top of the freelance translation market. I know at least two thriving freelancers who've told me they charge that much, plus several more translators who I suspect/assume charge that much. I should say for the purposes of this post that I don't earn 40 cents a word (for reasons I'll go into...). I do publish my rates, and on official document translations I do sometimes make up to a dollar a word when the project is priced per page.

First, let's give this number some context. If you produce, let's say 500 finished words an hour, 40 cents a word translates (so to speak) into $200 an hour. No question, that's good money. However, even here in Colorado (where professional services generally cost a lot less than in New York, LA, Chicago, etc.), my accountant makes $200 an hour and my business attorney makes $250.

The Wall Street Journal recently ran an article about the growing contingent of attorneys who charge over $1,000 an hour (yes, that's three zeros after the one). The article concludes with a prediction that within five to seven years, the gold standard for attorneys' fees will be an hour. So I think that part of the high rates issue is that if you want to charge 40 cents a word, you have to position yourself as a professional service provider on the level of an attorney, accountant, business strategy consultant etc. Realistically, most translators either cannot or are not willing to do that. Note that the WSJ article includes some excellent advice from an attorney who charges $1,100 an hour: "Some clients do focus on the hourly rate, but in the end what really matters is their total cost and whether they got a fair price." Good tip for any professional service provider!

Second, I would hazard a guess that many translators who charge very high rates work very slowly, or at least more slowly than translators who charge 10 cents a word. At 10 cents a word, you don't have the luxury of waiting for inspiration: you churn it out and send it in. At 40 cents per word, you have more of that luxury, and your clients also expect much more from your work. So maybe you produce 300, even 200 finished words an hour.

Third, as luscious as 40 cents a word might look, there are some reasons you might not want to charge that much:

- As Chris and others commented in relation to my previous

post, clients who pay 40-50 cents per word expect you to have their backs, all the time and with no exceptions. You cannot get huffy when there's a problem with your translation. You cannot shut off your phone and go hiking when that client is having a business meltdown. You must be cheerful, helpful and positive all the time. You must follow the news in that client's industry and spend your own money to go to their industry conferences whether or not they have a job in the pipeline for you. You must get out of your sweats and put on a suit and take that client to lunch a few times a year, shut up about yourself and invite them to talk about themselves. You must either take very short vacations or have someone you really, really trust who will fill in when you go away for more than a couple of days. In short, that $200 per hour is not going to come in exchange for only a modicum of effort on your part. And not to rant, but if some translators will not even spend $25 on business cards that don't have the "Get your free business cards!" text on the back, they are not going to do what's required to find and retain $200 an hour clients.

- Some specializations just don't pay that much (or at least this is what I tell myself!). For example, my preferred specialization is international development. I translate a lot of legal documents and I enjoy that work, but development is my real passion. And realistically, even high-level direct clients in those specializations probably do not have the budget to pay 40-50 cents a word on a regular basis. Realistically, even at the rates I charge now, I am probably paid more than a lot of the in-house employees at the companies I work for. However, I love the work, and I love translating documents that are, for lack of a less hackneyed way to put it, meaningful. So there's that aspect too.

None of this is to say that a) high income is a bad thing or b) 40-50 cents a word isn't worth striving for. Mostly, I wanted to raise the possibility that 40-50 cents a word is doable!

8.3 Some thoughts on hourly and salaried pay

In the early days of Thoughts on Translation (March, 2008 to be exact), I wrote a post on charging by the word versus charging by the hour. For a long time, it was the most active post on my blog and it inspired some interesting and heated discussion. Get Rich Slowly (`www.getrichslowly.org`) recently ran a post on hourly versus salaried jobs and it got me thinking about this issue again.

The translation industry complicates this issue in a couple of ways:

- We're normally paid by the word, rather than by the hour

- For whatever reason, most translation agencies will pay much more per word than per hour (in relative terms, not just absolute terms)

- Most of us don't rigorously track our output, so we don't really know how much we make per hour

- We usually work from home, so the client has only a vague idea of how long a given job takes us

Confused yet?

My first job in the translation industry was as an FBI contract linguist; a job that pays by the hour. Looking back, I see some advantages and disadvantages. On the up side, there's much less incentive to rush through a translation when you know that whether you produce 1,000 words an hour or 100 words an hour, you get paid the same amount. I think that a lot of translators use the per-word payment model as a rationale for doing a less than thorough job: why take an hour to research one term if you're getting paid 15, 20 or even 50 cents for it? When you're paid by the hour, you don't have that egg timer full of pennies hanging over your head and you can take as long as the translation requires.

However, being paid by the hour removes the translator's incentive to work more efficiently. In the comments on my original post, a few people pointed out that while there may be a fairly narrow range of per-word rates in our industry, experienced translators undoubtedly earn more than beginners (even if they charge the same amount per word) because they work much faster. Translators might be motivated to learn new software or to focus in a very specialized area because they know that their speed, and thus their income, will go up.

The confusing part of this is the disparity between the per-word and hourly rates that our industry will bear. For example, if a translator works with agencies, charges 15 cents per word and produces 500 finished words per hour, he/she is earning $75 an hour; and I think that both of those figures are realistic for experienced translators. But I have yet to hear of an agency that will pay $75 an hour for projects that are billed hourly; if I had to hazard a guess at the average agency rate (not a pricing recommendation, just my unscientific guess), I would say $35-$50 per hour is more common.

At an ATA conference years ago, I attended an excellent presentation on business practices by Jonathan Hine. His argument for charging by the hour for editing is that it's a zero loss-risk situation. Rather than taking the risk of receiving a poor translation and re-translating it for 4 cents a word, the editor can charge by the hour and be guaranteed of being compensated for all of the time that the edit takes. Maybe the reverse phenomenon is at work here; agencies would rather pay a higher per-word rate for translation, because then they know exactly how much the job will cost?

8.4 What about TM discounts?

During the recent discussion on volume discounts, a number of readers brought up the (very valid) issue of translation memory discounts. I feel a can of worms about to open here, but I'll inject some of my thoughts on TM discounts.

First caveat: I am neither a huge fan of nor a heavy user of TM. I own and use Trados Studio, OmegaT and Wordfast, and I really like all of them for different reasons. However because my favorite kind of work is translation that requires excellent writing, I only use TM when necessary. I find that because of the "chunked" nature of working in a TM tool, the flow of my writing really suffers when I use one. I do gain a pretty significant speed advantage when using TM, but I find that if the document needs to sound really natural in English, the extra editing time eats up the time I saved during the translation.

That being said, there are some projects where it would be suicidal not to use a TM. I work on several recurring projects for international development entities. These might involve multiple countries submitting funding applications using the same template, so it would be a huge waste of time to start each application from scratch. In those cases, I'm all about TM leverage.

There are two basic sides to the TM discount debate:

- Agency says: if some of the content in this document is recycled from a TM that we provide, why should we pay the translator's full rate for the recycled portion? The TM is the result of work that we paid for originally, so we want to realize the benefit of it.

- Translator says: I purchased the TM tool and used my own time to learn to use it. I pay for the upgrades and for the computer system that runs the TM. The time that I save by using the TM is a result of this investment, and I want to realize the benefit of it.

Over the years, I've struggled with the issue of TM discounts. In some specializations (i.e. software and documentation), the situation may be different from what I experience. But I find that editing fuzzy matches (i.e. anything below 100%) takes at least as long and sometimes longer than just translating the segment from scratch. Therefore, the only TM discount that I offer is that if the client is extremely confident in the reliability of the TM that they provide, I will not charge for 100% matches if I accept them without proofreading them. Meaning that in Wordfast Classic, if a segment shows up green (Wordfast's color code for a 100% match), I just click Alt-down (Wordfast's command for accepting a segment) without reading it. I feel that for clients who put in the work to maintain a reliable TM, this is a fair compromise. But because I've run the numbers on the time it takes to edit fuzzy matches, I don't offer TM discounts other than this.

8.5 Some thoughts on volume discounts

I get lots of questions from beginning and experienced translators about volume discounts (charging a lower per-word or hourly rate for larger projects). I actually think that after "how much should I charge?," "should I offer a volume discount" might be the second most frequently-asked question that I see.

When I first started translating, I enthusiastically offered volume discounts. During my first year as a freelancer I worked about 10 hours a week and made $9,000. Seriously- there's no zero missing! Out of that $9,000, $2,000 came from just one project on which I gave a substantial volume discount. Why? Because I didn't have much work, and working for less than my standard rate was a lot more appealing than not working at all. Flash forward nine years, and I recently realized that not only do I not offer a volume discount any more, but sometimes I actually impose what might be considered a volume surcharge. Why? Because I have enough work at my standard rates and a volume discount would put me in the position of turning down other projects at my standard rate. However, I will sometimes do a small project at a lower rate as a favor to one of my regular clients. It helps them out, it doesn't tie up too much of my time at a lower rate and it shows the client that I'm willing to show some flexibility within reasonable limits.

Volume discounts have their place. I think that the principle of volume discounts is fair: if a client guarantees you a week or two of work, you get to spend all of that time on the clock. Your administrative overhead is a lot lower, because you're dealing with one client and one invoice rather than 10 clients and 10 invoices. You will probably work faster as you "ramp up" on the project rather than switching gears twice a day. You don't have to stress out about juggling multiple projects because you're just plugging away on The Big One. But when your client base grows, you have less of an incentive to offer a volume discount: you're not desperate for the work, you're busy most or all of the time anyway, and if you're too busy, it's time to raise your rates!

8.6 Supplier or demander?

When it comes to raising your translation rates, what's the correct strategy: ask or tell? A colleague and I talked about this at length today, and it struck me as good food for thought.

In one sense, other professional service providers don't phone you up and ask if it's OK with you if they raise their rates. When you go to get your teeth cleaned or your taxes done, it generally costs more than the last time you went, but most of us simply accept this without question. We don't haggle with the dentist about why a cleaning has gone from $150 to $175 in six months, we just write out the check or hand over the credit card and pay the bill. It would seem odd if these service providers made too much of an issue about rates; if I called my accountant and he said "Just to let you know, I'm now charging $10 an hour more than last year, do you still want to come in?" it would give me pause, not because of the money but because of his calling so much attention to a relatively small increase.

Clearly, these people view themselves as suppliers, and as such they raise their rates without consulting their clients. The mobile computer support consultant doesn't call us up and ask if we'll stick with him if he charges 25% more, and the bookkeeper doesn't solicit our input before upping her fees; they just do it, and we decide whether to continue using them or not.

Translation is a little different. While the average dentist's or accountant's or bookkeeper's income base is probably made up of hundreds or even thousands of clients, each of whose contribution to the service provider's income is relatively small, the average freelance translator probably has fewer than 10 regular clients, and may even earn 50% or more of his/her income from one or two major clients. For a translator, the loss of a major client can be catastrophic, or at the very least result in a need to quickly find new clients to make up for the loss of income.

In our industry, it's also not uncommon for the rates we charge longstanding clients to fall behind the rates we charge new clients. Most of us are as busy as or busier than we want to be, so it's not much of a risk to quote new clients a higher rate than what our existing clients pay. But when we reach a situation where a major client is paying substantially less than our other clients, do we: a) take the dentist's approach and simply start issuing invoices for a higher amount without saying anything, b) ask the client if they will agree to a raise, explaining that we're now charging everyone else more than what we charge them, c) notify the client that as of X date, our rate is increasing, or d) another approach entirely?

I think that translators resist increasing their rates with existing clients partially because our per-word pay amounts are so small compared to a yearly salary. If we had a salaried job, most of us would see a $2,000 raise as real money, something worth haggling over. But if you translate 200,000 words a year for your top clients, a raise of 1 cent per word comes out to that same $2,000; a raise of 2 cents per word would put $4,000 in your pocket. So I think that too often, we avoid increasing our rates with longstanding clients because we tell ourselves that "it's only 1,2,3 cents per word," when in fact that adds up to a lot of money.

In the conversation today with my colleague, one barometer we came up with is our replacement value with our existing clients. For example, could those clients replace us with a translator of similar skill level at the same rates we charge? With some clients, the answer is clearly yes. If we're honest, I think that most of us will admit that sometimes, we lob out a higher than usual rate because it's Friday afternoon and we need some time off, or because we're overworked and don't feel like negotiating, and the client says yes anyway. In other cases, the answer is clearly no; we're giving a client great work and fast turnaround times at below market rates, and we need to make a balanced business decision on when and how to try to change things.

8.7 Some thoughts on translation rates

Rates are possibly the most personal and contentious issue in the translation industry. Some translators are very open about what they charge, while others don't like to talk about it at all. Some translators feel that competitive pricing is the way to go while others would rather aim for the highest rates that the market will bear.

For my regular clients, I provide a rate sheet and I guarantee those rates for one calendar year. I feel that this is important because agencies have many more fixed expenses than I do, such as office rent, employee salaries, tech support, software upgrades, etc. and I want to give them a firm price that they can depend on. On the other hand, when a new or unknown client contacts me, the rate I offer depends on various factors: the nature of the work, the deadline, and to be honest, how much I want or need the job. This is also how I test out a raise in rates; if I quote a higher rate than my standard one and the new client accepts it without negotiation, I know that the market will probably start to bear that new rate.

When setting my rates, I take various factors into account. For example, clients who pay quickly, always pay on time and are very easy to work with get a preferred rate because my collection and hassle overhead is almost nothing. I do the translation, the client rarely questions my work and I'm paid promptly and in full. For clients such as this, I feel that it's worth offering a competitive rate because I then rise to the top of their list of translators and am offered a lot of work from them.

The best time to try to raise your rates is when you are very busy, because you're less concerned with landing the job. My informal system is that when I am very busy and get a call from a new client, I ask for the rate that will make the job worth my time, and if the client doesn't accept it, that's OK. If a particular project really interests me or fits a specific time slot I'm looking to fill (for example I could complete it during a "working vacation").

8.8 Paid by the word or paid by the hour

At last year's American Translators Association conference in San Francisco, I overheard a few conversations about how the translation industry would be affected if translators started billing by the hour rather than by the word. In some cases and for some jobs, translators do bill by the hour, but the tried-and-true per-word charge is still the norm. Here are a few thoughts on charging by the word versus by the hour.

Pricing translation by the word has some advantages: Especially if you charge by the source word, everyone knows up front how much the translation will cost, down to the cent. No surprise overruns to deal with and no estimating how many hours a project will take. Per-word pricing encourages translators to maintain their skills and technology, since efficient translators effectively earn more per hour. In some sense, per-word pricing may also drive translation technology innovations, since translators may be more likely to purchase a tool that allows them to work faster. Also, skilled and efficient translators can probably earn more by charging by the word than clients would be likely to pay by the hour. Say that you're translating 600 words an hour at 14 cents a word: I'll venture a guess that those same clients might balk at paying $84 an hour for translation. Per-word pricing also allows translation buyers to compare apples to apples when it comes to costs, rather than weighing a higher per-hour quote from a translator who claims to work faster versus a lower per-hour quote from someone who works more slowly.

But then again...:Pricing by the word has an obvious disadvantage from the translator's side, which is that you are agreeing to work for a flat and fixed rate. So, when you get to those three pages of barely legible handwriting, or the document that's been scanned, faxed and photocopied eight times before arriving in your inbox, you have to decide whether you need to negotiate a higher per-word rate. This can be a particular problem when it comes to editing, which is why I personally decline to be paid by the word for editing.

So then maybe pricing by the hour is better?: Well... yes... no...

maybe! The main advantage of pricing by the hour is that there is no risk of loss on the translator's part; if you charge $50 an hour and you work ten hours, you make $500. If you charge 20 cents a word and think you can translate 600 words an hour but the nature of the document is such that you really translate 250 words an hour, you've just taken a big hit. However, my main reasons for continuing to believe in pricing by the word are: a) the client knows up front how much the translation will cost and b) I think that most experienced and efficient translators can earn more by the word than what most clients will pay by the hour. Just don't forget to agree in advance on whether the billable word count is source or target!

8.9 Payments without borders

When a translator and a translation client are located in different countries, the usual issues that have to be resolved with payments (rate, payment terms, etc.) are joined by an additional question, that of the payment method. From the perspective of a U.S.-based translator, here are a few international payment method options and some of the pros and cons that I've found:

- Check in U.S. dollars. Some larger international agencies have either a branch in the U.S. or an account denominated in dollars. No problem here!

- Wire transfer into the translator's U.S. account. Pro: Relatively uncomplicated, each party can pay their own fees. Con: Fees for incoming and outgoing fees vary by bank. I have my business account with Chase bank and they charge $15 for an incoming foreign wire transfer. Some credit unions don't charge at all, and I've seen fees as high as $50 for incoming foreign transfers.

- PayPal. Pro: Easy to set up, can bill the client in various currencies, various ways for the client to fund the payment. Con: Fees vary dramatically from zero for a domestic eCheck to up to 5% for foreign credit cards. I learned this the hard way when I ended up paying $150 to receive $3,000 from an overseas client. I had been chasing them for the money for a while and didn't want to reject the payment, but the size of the fee really turned me off using PayPal for large transactions since you sometimes can't control how the client funds them.

- Overseas bank account. Pro: Easier for the client, can allow the translator to hold the money in a country he/she visits, gives the translator more control over how and when the money is transferred into a U.S. account. Con: Can be difficult to set up if you need a business account and are not a citizen of the non-U.S. country. After lengthy negotiations with two international commercial banks, I decided that this option was simply too complex and costly to be worth pursuing for the amount of European clients I have.

- Depositing foreign currency checks into a U.S. account. Pro: Easy for the client, client does not incur any fees. Con: Some banks (including the Chase branch I deal with) absolutely won't accept foreign currency checks; checks may be sent back to the country of issue for collection before being credited to your account, or the exchange rate may be poor.

8.10 Tracking your freelance income

After reading Jill Sommer's post on job tracking systems for freelancers (www.translationmusings.com), I thought I would write something about income tracking systems.

As with job tracking systems, there are various ways to track your income and outstanding invoices. I used to use a white board to write down the details of every invoice I issued. I liked this system because it kept everything in front of my eyes, and it was easy to see when invoices were overdue. There are also various programs such as Translation Office 3000 that will track your invoices and income as well. TO3000 isn't cheap (150 euros), but I think I might buy it if they produced a Linux version (yes, that's a hint!). I've always used the open source accounting software GnuCash for my business accounting, and I've been quite happy with it.

I abandoned my white board invoice tracking system because I wanted a way to track my total outstanding invoices. Although this is obviously possible using the white board system and a calculator, it's much easier if you use a spreadsheet, because you can just write a sum formula for the upper (or lower) cell in the column where you record the invoice amounts. My thought on this was that by tracking my total outstanding invoices (and assuming that clients pay on time, which most of mine thankfully do!), I would have an objective data point on which to base my project acceptance decisions. For example, if I want to earn a gross amount of $6,000 a month and I see that I currently have only $4,500 in outstanding invoices, I know that I can't be picky about accepting new work. On the other hand, if I have $7,000 outstanding, I know that I have at least a week of wiggle room and I can afford to either plan some days off or work on non-paying projects such as my blog, book and translation-related volunteer work.

I use a simple OpenOffice spreadsheet (like an Excel sheet) and record the invoice number in the A column, the issue date in the B column, the client in the C column, the invoice amount in the D column (and the top cell in the D column is the sum of all of the D cells below it) and the date paid in the E column. In the E column I also record follow-up to any overdue invoices i.e. "first reminder sent 6/5" or "certified letter with request for payment within 30 days sent 5/5."

I find this system useful because it's easy; every time I issue an invoice, I just record the details in the spreadsheet, and when I receive a payment, I delete the entry for that invoice so that it's no longer included in my outstanding total. Also, this system makes it very easy to see whether I'm reaching my income goals; "no paid vacation" is one of the elements of freelancing that's quite different from a salaried job, and often the major cost of a vacation is not the trip itself but the loss of income associated with it. I find that using an income tracking system helps me objectively decide when I need to hit the grindstone and when I can afford to spend an afternoon outdoors!

8.11 Some thoughts on financial management

After working all day on my business taxes (year-end and fourth quarter... I need a mocha!), my thoughts are firmly stuck in the financial realm. So let's stick with that topic and talk about some tips for managing your freelance finances. Some of these are US-specific and some apply worldwide.

- Have a business bank account and business debit card. Your business and personal finances should be completely separate, and the debit card statements save you from dealing with a shoebox full of receipts at the end of the year.

- I posted this one on Twitter earlier today. Set up a business savings account. Every time you receive a payment from a client, immediately transfer at least 30% of the payment into the savings account (the exact amount depends on your tax bracket, retirement goals, etc.). Use the saved funds to pay your taxes, fund your retirement account, etc. Over the years, I've heard numerous freelancers lamenting "...made more money than I thought this year... owe $6,000 and I don't know where that's coming from..." This year-end downer can easily be avoided with the business savings account plan.

- Keep a running total of your receivables. Let's say that your gross income goal is $6,000 per month. If you only have $4,000 in outstanding invoices, it's time to get cracking; you can't afford to be too picky about what you accept and what you decline. If you have $8,000 in outstanding invoices, it's a good time to raise your rates, be choosier about what you accept, or work on some non-paying projects that interest you. I use an Excel spreadsheet for this task. Whenever

I issue an invoice, I enter it into the Excel sheet and it is automatically added to my running total receivables.

- Set up a paid vacation account. Lots of translators insist that they can never take time off because if they don't work, they don't get paid. Part of the solution is to raise your rates so that you don't have to be working all the time. The other part is to give yourself paid vacation. For example if you typically gross $1,500 per week and you want to take 4 weeks a year off, you need $6,000 in savings in order to pay yourself $1,500 per week off. Divided by the 48 weeks a year that you would be working, that's $125 per week. Stash that amount in your paid vacation account and when your vacation time rolls around, you're set!

- If you subcontracted more than $600 of work to anyone during the year, make sure to send that person/entity a 1099-MISC by January 31. I use FileTaxes.com to prepare these online and mail them to the recipients. My accountant recommends sending 1099s to both individuals and corporations.

- Within the limits of the law, deduct, deduct, deduct. I've been freelancing for 10 years and I'm still finding out about new deductions: this year's discovery was the potential to deduct my daughter's summer day camp costs (may apply to private babysitting too) under the Federal child care credit. Some restrictions apply: the child has to be under 13, sleepaway fees are not eligible, and if you are married, your spouse has to be employed. Plus, of course there's a cap: you can probably claim only $3,000 per child or $6,000 total, and that includes work-related child care during the school year if you use any. And as always, ask your accountant!

8.12 ATA conference topic: low payers

Amazingly enough in this economy, my sense from the Denver ATA conference is that most freelancers are very happy with their work volume and income levels. Especially as compared with the gloom and doom of the US economy (maybe even the world economy?), I think we're doing quite well. This year has brought me as much work as I wanted and I'm happy with my income despite devoting a fair bit of time to the second edition of my book and my new webinar venture.

Still, low-paying agencies were a hot topic at the conference. Some freelancers feel that ATA should take a stand on this or somehow get involved (not likely to happen in any case), or that freelancers should come to some sort of consensus on how to handle these agencies. I don't have the perfect answer, but here are some of my thoughts, and feel free to add your own:

- The best defense against low payers is simply to be too busy to even contemplate working with them. When I receive lowball inquiries from agencies, I either delete them without responding or respond and say "My minimum rate is X and I'm very busy at that rate, so I will have to decline. Please keep me in mind if you have any future projects with a larger budget." Part of me feels that an agency looking for a professional translator for 6 cents a word doesn't even deserve a response, while the other part of me feels that it's a public service to communicate that professionals charge real money and that we are very busy dealing with clients who pay real money.

- There really is enough well-paying work to go around. Judy Jenner says this all the time, and I completely agree. There is more than enough well-paying work for all 2,000 people who were at the ATA conference and then some. Leave the low payers to their business model while you pursue yours: the market is there.

- Most translators charge what their work is worth. You know how every once in a while you have this horrible sinking fear that there are people out there charging a tiny fraction of what you charge and producing well-researched, beautifully-written translations delivered on or before deadline with a smile? Well, I would let go of that fear. As demonstrated by Chris Durban's "Mystery Shopper" experiment (described in her presentation at the ATA Translation Company Division conference), agencies that compete on price alone generally produce unusably lousy translations, using some combination of non-native speakers, people who aren't actually professional translators, machine translation or all three.

- If you don't want to deal with low payers, step away from the places they hang out. I'm not one to name names, but auction-style translation marketplaces are not the place to be if you want to earn real money. Instead, market to quality-conscious agencies: see my post on Using Payment Practices as a marketing tool for some ideas on how to do that.

- Don't expect associations to get involved. It's not really ATA's place to disrupt the free market or set freelancers' rates for them. Even if ATA were legally able to get involved in rates, who gets to decide what constitutes lowballing? If you currently work for 15 cents a word, 7 cents is lowballing. If you currently work for 45 cents a word, 30 cents is lowballing, and so on.

- Put your energy where it matters. I believe in fighting for what's right, but you're never going to put the Wal-Marts of translation out of business or convince them to quadruple what they pay their translators. So move on; let go. You know how they say that living well is the best revenge? Get your revenge on the lowball market by charging more than they will ever be able to!

In general, I can't say that I spend a lot of time thinking about or dealing with the Wal-Marts of translation. They're not my target market and I have more than enough work without them.

9 Webinar questions

The articles in this section answer questions that were submitted by attendees from a series of webinars that I presented in late 2010 and early 2011.

9.1 Small-diffusion languages

A participant asks: Do you have any advice for small (exotic) language translators? My native language is Hungarian.

Short answer: Hmm. Tough to answer this in one sentence. Let's move on to the longer answer.

Longer answer: First, how small is too small when it comes to small-diffusion languages? My sense is that there is enough of a market for Hungarian and similarly-sized languages to support a freelancer. For example, Hungarian is one of the 23 official languages of the European Union. That alone would seem to generate a fair bit of work, since any industry that is regulated in the EU (i.e. pharmaceuticals and medical devices) is required to produce product information in the official languages. However I do think that some languages are just so small/exotic that there may not be enough work to support a freelancer unless you really know where to look. For example, I once talked to a project manager at a fairly large agency who happened to be a native speaker of Albanian. She told me that in her multi-year tenure with that agency, she had never seen an Albanian project come through their pipeline. But let's say that you translate a language that is small (i.e. Hungarian) but large enough that you can make a go of it as a translator. Here are some ideas:

- Team up with other translators and form a small, single-language agency. Many large agencies probably struggle to deal with high-volume projects in, say, Hungarian. While a medium to large agency can probably assemble a German (French, Spanish, etc.) team to translate 100,000 words in a week, they may panic when they have to deal with a similar situation in Hungarian, Slovene or Maltese. So by forming a small team of translators, you could be a one-stop shop for other, larger agencies. Instead of spending a whole day on the phone trying to find eight Greek translators who are available for two weeks, the larger agencies could just call you.

- Find clients who really need you. Various sources have said that the European Commission can only meet 70% of its demand for Romanian, Latvian and Maltese interpreting because it cannot find enough qualified candidates. Especially if you translate one of the EU official languages, European governmental entities are probably a good target.

- Be open to a variety of subject areas. Beginning French, German and Spanish translators are often advised to specialize as narrowly as possible in order to differentiate themselves in a crowded market. My instinct about smaller-diffusion languages would be the opposite: especially if you're going to accept outsourced work from larger agencies, you probably need to accept a wide range of subject areas.

9.2 How many words per day?

A participant asks: For a translator who doesn't use CAT tools, what is the average turnaround/output in words per day?

Short answer: If you want to work for agencies, you probably need to translate 2,000-3,000 words per day in order to meet their deadlines. If you work for direct clients, you can work more at your own pace. I know translators who average anywhere between 200 and 1,000 finished words per hour, so obviously your mileage will vary!

Longer answer: First, I'm not completely convinced that CAT tools save translators a lot of time unless the project is extremely repetitive (i.e. updating a previously translated document). When I use WordFast or OmegaT, I find that my translation speed increases by about 10% because I'm not constantly finding my place in the source document and glancing back and forth between screens, but I also find that my editing time increases because my writing is more "chunked" and does not flow as well. I avoid using CAT tools on anything that is for publication, but that's another post!

If I had to put a number on it, I would say that the average translator produces between 400 and 600 finished words per hour. However, most people can't translate for 8 hours without stopping, and most of the time you'll encounter a section in the document that you have to research or read about, so you'll slow down. In addition, most translators' work speed varies enormously depending on the subject matter and format of the document. Years ago I used to translate market research surveys that were so repetitive I could listen to audio books while I worked and still produce about 800 finished words per hour. However, this also meant that the work was not very stimulating/fulfilling/intellectually demanding and therefore not very satisfying. I've worked on really complex legal documents that involved multiple cross-references and layers of meaning, and I've dipped as low as 250 words per hour.

As I mentioned in the short answer to this question, I think that agencies expect that translators will produce 2,000 to 3,000 finished words per day, and in general you have to be able to translate that fast in order to make a healthy income on agency rates (of course there are exceptions!). I'm not in the "faster is better" camp, but if you want to translate faster, you could:

- Work on your typing. It sounds simplistic, but a lot of translators could translate faster if they typed faster. Recently, someone doing a research project on translators' typing speeds asked me to take a typing speed test. I scored 83 words a minute (eternal thanks to my 10th grade keyboarding teacher!); according to the typing website, this means that I save 5.5 hours per 10 hours of typing as compared with "the average typist" who does 36 words per minute. Moral: typing speed matters!

- Use speech recognition software or hire a transcriptionist. Most speech recognition software and most transcriptionists should be able to handle 80-120 words per minute. If you're at that 36 word per minute average, this could really increase your productivity. I haven't tried speech recognition software because I just don't think that fast! And I don't mind typing. But most of the ultra-productive translators I know (800-1,000 words per hour) do use speech recognition software.

- Concentrate on your specializations. I think that the best way to increase your translation speed is to become really knowledgeable about your areas of specialization and stick to them. Once you start to know the terminology, sentence structure, typical phrasing, and even your regular clients' writing styles, you'll really speed up.

9.3 Preparing for the American Translators Association certification exams

A participant asks: How can I prepare for the American Translators Association certification exam?

Short answer: Order a practice test from ATA; at $50 (including return of the graded copy of your exam) as opposed to $300 for the real exam (not including return of the graded copy of your exam), it's a good investment and a good indicator of your chances of passing the real exam.

Longer answer: If you'd like to take the ATA exam, you need to do a few things:

- Join ATA (www.atanet.org)

- Read the "Certification" section of ATA's website and make sure you meet the eligibility requirements for the exam. If you don't meet them and you do not currently work as a translator, your most expeditious route is probably to get a translation certificate from an approved program; there's a list on the ATA website.

- Gather (buy, borrow, check out of the library) enough paper dictionaries and reference books for the exam. At present, ATA does not allow candidates to use any electronic resources for the exam, but you can use all of the paper dictionaries that you can carry. When I took the test, the woman next to me brought a rolling suitcase full of dictionaries covering a variety of subject areas.

- Familiarize yourself with the error marking framework for the exam, the tips for candidates and the other resources on ATA's website.

- Take a practice test and see how you do. You can order a practice test from the "Certification" section of the ATA website. The magic number is 17; with 17 or fewer error points, you're in. If you take the practice test and get 20 error points, you probably have a chance of passing the real exam (this happened to me) but if you get 40 error points, well...

And a few random thoughts on the ATA exam:

- I am ATA-certified and find it to be a boost for my business. At the very least, someone browsing the ATA online directory is likely to call the certified translators first. I do a pretty brisk business translating official documents for individual direct clients, partially because I'm one of only three ATA-certified French to English translators in Colorado. However, the highest paid freelancers I know, people in the 40+ cents per word market, are not certified. You can definitely earn a very healthy income as a freelance translator without being certified.

- As discussed on Jill Sommer's blog (translationmusings. com), there are lots of issues with the ATA exam. The hand-

writing factor is huge; personally I don't hand-write anything except my grocery list, and I found it excruciating
to hand write the whole exam. In nearly a decade as a
freelancer, I have never hand-written a translation other
than the ATA exam. Ditto with paper dictionaries; most
of us have moved over to entirely electronic terminology
resources and it's tough to translate without using them.
When I took the exam, the general passage was much, much
harder than the specialized passage, and I felt that the grading standards were heavily swayed toward a fairly literal,
word-by-word translation; the kind of translation I try to
avoid when I translate for publication. ATA is working on
a lot of these issues. And to be fair, it's hard to deal with
some of them (for example the long turnaround time to get
your exam graded) without raising the price beyond most
translators' means.

- The pass rate for the ATA certification exams is very low.
  ATA does not release exact statistics, but the pass rate seems
  to be about 20%. However: a) this is comparable to, or even
  higher than the pass rates for similar exams such as the
  Federal Court Interpreter certification exam. Some court
  interpreter certification exams even have a pass rate around
  5%. b) if you fail the ATA exam, it means that two separate
  graders agree that you failed. Every exam is reviewed by
  two graders to start out with. If they disagree on the result,
  the exam is then sent to another grader for a third review.
  So you cannot fail the exam based on only one person's
  assessment of your test. c) I would be interested to see the
  pass rates broken down by language. Anecdotally, it seems
  that some languages' pass rates are much lower than others

- If I were to give ATA some business advice, I would advise
  them to start producing preparation materials for the certification exams. I think that this would serve the twofold
  purpose of making the exam and the grading process more
  transparent and of generating revenue for ATA. For example, ATA could publish preparation manuals of old exams

with graded example translations. They could even offer preparation courses. Hey, if people will spend several thousand dollars for a bar exam preparation course, ATA should be able to charge real money for a translator certification exam preparation course.

9.4 Should I incorporate?

A participant asks: As a self-employed freelance translator, should I operate as an LLC, an S-corp or a sole proprietorship?

Short answer: If you freelance full-time, I think it's worth incorporating. As long as you don't mind the extra paperwork, incorporating has some significant tax and liability advantages.

Longer answer: First, I'm not an accountant or an attorney. Second, I have an S-corp so I'm more informed about S-corps than about LLCs and C-corps. Third, I can't speak to tax issues in countries other than the U.S. That being said:

- Running your freelance business as a sole proprietor is really simple; just report your freelance income on IRS Schedule C, pay self-employment tax on it and you're pretty much set. Running a corporation is a little more complicated: you may have to file monthly or quarterly payroll taxes and a separate end-of-year corporate tax return. You will have to pay to register your corporation every year and the IRS may be less lenient with you than with a sole proprietor if you mess up your taxes. If you don't want to be bothered with any extra paperwork or filing requirements, stick with sole proprietorship.

- The hassle factor of incorporating depends on the state in which you live, since corporations are registered at the state level. Here in Colorado, incorporating is very simple and cheap but you do have to renew your corporate registration every year. Check your state's Secretary of State website for the requirements where you live.

- The tax advantages of incorporating can be significant. When you work as a sole proprietor, you pay self-employment tax (currently 15.30%) on everything you earn, minus your business expenses. This is in addition to the normal Federal rate that you would pay if you worked for an employer, so it's a big hit. Some corporate structures allow you to take some of your earnings as "wages" which are subject to self-employment tax and some of your earnings as "profit" which is not subject to self-employment tax. My understanding is that this applies to S-corps and C-corps but not LLCs unless the LLC files taxes as an S-corp. So for example if you gross $70,000 and take $40,000 as wages and $30,000 as profit, you have the potential to save $4,590 in self-employment tax (15.3% x 30,000). Even if you do quarterly payroll taxes (mine take about an hour per quarter) and pay an accountant to file your corporate tax return, this is a big win.

- Liability: I have never heard of a lawsuit against a freelance translator, but the U.S. is the most litigious country in the world so it's certainly not out of the question. Incorporating separates your business and personal assets; if you're sued, the plaintiff can only go after your business' assets and not your house, car or personal bank accounts. If you're a sole proprietor, your personal assets are theoretically fair game if you are sued for a business issue.

- Incorporating seems to make you less likely to be audited by the IRS. It's a bit hard to pin down the exact statistics, but articles by respected tax professionals such as Barbara Weltman suggest that audit rates for S-corps are dramatically lower than those for sole proprietors. Weltman states that the total S-corp audit rate is 0.4% and the audit rate for Schedule C filers earning between $100,000 and $200,000 per year is 3.9%.

9.5 Does age matter?

A participant asks: Can one be too old to begin a translation business (for example, as indicated by degree completion years) or do prospective employers generally not care?

Short answer: As a freelancer, I wouldn't worry about age too much. If you're up-to-date enough to participate in a webinar and even submit a question, I think you're fine.

Longer answer: This worry applies to both ends of the spectrum: 22 year old new graduates and 68 year old retirees often ask "Will clients take me seriously?" In both cases, I think the answer is "yes," if you keep a few important factors in mind:

- As a group, freelance translators aren't that young. Case in point: I'm 39 and have an 8 year old child, and I'm regularly referred to as a "girl" or "young lady" by elder members of the profession. The oldest freelancer I've heard of was in his early 90s and I know of numerous successful freelancers in the 70+ bracket.

- Degree completion years? For a US resumé, I'd leave them off. After all, age discrimination is illegal and as long as you can do the job, your clients really don't need to know how old you are. Likewise, I know several translators in their 60s and beyond who deliberately do not put their photo on their marketing materials.

- Whether you're on the young or old end of the freelance spectrum, keep the negative stereotypes of your age group in mind and defy them. For example, take the stereotype that older workers are set in their ways and resist new technologies. Beat this image by pointing out that you've recently participated in a webinar (or even more than one!) for freelance translators, that you use Skype to communicate with your clients and colleagues and that you're really looking forward to getting to know your clients' preferences and style guidelines. If you're in your 20s, pay particular attention to being reliable, responsible and possibly more formal than you would be otherwise. For example, a conference interpreter training program director in the UK recently attributed the EU's difficulty in finding new into-English interpreters to the candidates' poor skills in their native language: Many of the young hopefuls cannot speak in the appropriate "register" for the event they would be interpreting. Their only modes of speech are informal, peppered with "like", for instance, she says. They misuse words and don't know the subtle differences between synonyms. So, brush up on your formal speaking skills before you go for the interview!

- For better or worse, freelance translation is a real meritocracy. On the one hand I think that most clients, at least in the US, are largely concerned with your ability to do a good job and don't really care if you're older or younger than they expected. On the other hand, one flubbed assignment can get you kicked to the electronic curb, so make sure to keep your focus on outstanding work.

Index

agencies, 15–20, 22–25, 31, 45–47, 89, 90, 115, 118, 122, 123, 128, 130, 135–139
American Translators Association, 27, 28, 30, 35, 37, 38, 40–42, 50, 89, 91, 108, 115, 117, 118, 123, 135, 136, 140–143

blogging, 7, 9, 36
business cards, 32, 41, 44, 111, 121

certification, 26, 27, 91, 140–143
clients, 11, 12, 14, 16, 17, 19–27, 33–36, 39, 40, 42–47, 49, 50, 53, 56, 59, 60, 66–69, 72–75, 77–80, 82, 83, 85, 86, 89, 90, 93, 94, 97, 98
cold calling, 34
cold contacting, 11, 12
cover letter, 12

e-mail, 11–13, 16, 17, 22–24, 30, 34, 37, 38, 42, 50, 64, 65, 82, 84, 85, 91, 94, 95, 103, 104, 107, 109, 112, 113

informational interview, 13, 19
interpreters, 24, 28, 30, 31, 50, 117, 118, 146

marketing, 18, 22, 25, 26, 33–36, 39, 40, 44, 45, 64, 69, 70, 75, 78, 79, 88, 110, 111, 113, 136, 145

netbook, 102–104

Payment Practices, 18, 91, 93, 136

phone, 11
phone calls, 11, 19, 24, 94, 98, 115
proofreading, 22, 51–53, 124

rates, 19, 20, 29, 40, 42, 43, 45, 46, 53, 79, 80, 85–87, 89, 90, 115, 120, 121, 123, 125–128, 133, 134, 136, 139, 142, 144
referral, 11, 78, 83
resumé, 11, 12, 15, 23, 28, 113–115, 145
rush charge, 20

Skype, 145
smartphone, 98, 102–104
spam, 12, 113
specialization, 11–16, 18, 26, 29, 34, 38, 43, 45, 46, 52, 57–60, 62, 66, 67, 81, 82, 89, 115, 121, 124
specializations, 140
startup phase, 13, 14, 46

translation memory, 104, 106, 107, 123

website, 12, 19, 21–23, 34, 36, 39, 44, 57, 71, 75, 89, 99, 100, 110, 112, 117, 139–141

About the author

Corinne McKay is an ATA-certified French to English translator based in Boulder, Colorado. Her blog, Thoughts on Translation, went live in February, 2008 and has since become a vibrant discussion forum for freelance translators around the world. Corinne's down-to-earth tips are based on her own experience building a successful translation business after a first career as a high school teacher. She is also the author of *How to Succeed as a Freelance Translator*, the original how-to guide for freelance translators, with over 5,000 copies in print.

Colophon

This book was produced entirely with free/open source software running on Debian Gnu/Linux. The text was written in OpenOffice.org Writer and typeset with LyX in the Palatino font.